TX
823
.H28
1989

Hamerstrom,
Frances, 1907-

Wild food cookbook

$17.95

DATE			

Wild Food Cookbook

Illustrated by Elva Hamerstrom Paulson

FRANCES HAMERSTROM

WILD
FOOD
COOKBOOK

IOWA STATE UNIVERSITY PRESS / AMES

BOOKS BY FRANCES HAMERSTROM

Adventure of the Stone Man

Walk When the Moon Is Full

An Eagle to the Sky

Strictly for the Chickens

Birds of Prey of Wisconsin

Birding with a Purpose

Harrier, Hawk of the Marshes

Wild Food Cookbook

Manufactured in the United States of America

First edition, 1989

Library of Congress Cataloging-in-Publication Data

Hamerstrom, Frances, 1907–
    Wild food cookbook / Frances Hamerstrom : illustrated by Elva
Hamerstrom Paulson. – 1st ed.
        p.   cm.
    Bibliography: p.
    Includes index.
    ISBN 0-8138-0116-8
        1. Cookery (Wild foods)   I. Title.
    TX823.H28   1989
    641.6 – dc19   88-25053
                                                          CIP

To Frederick—
who lent me his taste buds for 58 years

CONTENTS

SUMMER

AUTUMN

WINTER

PROLOGUE

A feeling of self sufficiency in wild country whether for a meal, a day, or days on end, is a delight and a personal triumph in applied natural history.

As a child I used to build daydreams of how I would manage if I found myself suddenly alone in a great forest. Sometimes I was the sole survivor from a shipwreck and sometimes I had fallen from a plane, miraculously unhurt, but with a jackknife in my pocket. I don't know what other little girls were thinking about when they stared out of the schoolroom window away in a world of their own, but for my part I might be fishing with a safety pin, snaring with a shoelace, or brewing mysterious teas to drink with my supper of nuts, berries, and herbs.

I did not suspect that scattered fragments of these childhood dreams would one day become part of my usual way of life; that a knack for living off the country would sometimes be a buffer against poverty, but more often it would mean freedom — to follow a flock of prairie chickens, the trail of a fox, or our own sweet whim, without dropping what we were doing for a mere bag of groceries.

It was in 1935 that Frederick and I first encountered canned "weeds." Lured by the drumming of a partridge, we came upon an opening with a cluster of buildings even more tumbledown than the abandoned farm we had just moved into. An old, old couple invited us in.

"Come in and sit. We've just celebrated our fifty-eighth wedding anniversary." They were handsome people — she little, merry, and quick like a chipmunk on her brown bare feet; he tall, almost gaunt, sizing us up with his one remaining eye.

Time-polished knots stood high on the floorboard which creaked under our weight. Supper was cooking on the wood range. The walls had been carefully papered — layer upon layer of newspaper — "Keeps the cold out and brightens up the kitchen." There were two stools, two rocking chairs and in the dim recesses of the big room, a large brass double bed. Rows and rows of full mason jars packed with a pale greenish substance were tidily stacked under the bed.

"Them's fiddleheads," she said, "greens for winter."

It was not until midwinter, however, that it dawned on me that there are people who are living off the country as a matter of course and from necessity, not just playing Indian or bringing in delicacies. In February our neighbor came to us. I don't know how he made it. Snow measured thirty-four inches on the level that winter, but it wasn't level; the drifts were piled high, in some places two thirds the height of the telephone poles. He had bucked the drifts on foot and stood suddenly at my kitchen door, one-eyed, almost frail in the wind, with icicles a-glitter in his beard. "My woman's sick. Can you get the doctor?"

It probably took me less time to cover the five and a half miles to town to get out the government plow so the doctor could get in, than it took the old gentleman to beat his way back through the woods and marshes to his sick wife. He wouldn't wait to ride the plow. Just as we parted I thought of those jars of pale greens under the brass bed; he didn't look much of a hand at cooking. "Take along a can of soup, it will give her strength." The old gentleman took the can from me and paused a moment, turning it slowly in his hands with great interest. At last he said, "Why, it's *sealed,* isn't it?"

That evening at supper, when Frederick had come in from the woods, I told him about my day. "Just think, they've been married fifty-eight years and never eaten out of a tin can!"

"That's funny," he said. "They had geraniums on their window sill and those geraniums were in tin cans."

It was spring when we stopped to see the old couple again. He was chopping wood and she was baking bread in the sunny kitchen. I asked her how it happened that she had tin cans to put her flowers in.

"Why, I found them."

From those who *find* tin cans, and *find* most of their food one can learn much—not only of delicious surprises, but more often of courage, ingenuity, and foods—some tasteless or of appalling monotony but also rare delicacies.

Those jars of greens under the bed opened our eyes. We were hungry most of the time then, and we learned that it *was* possible to find food! That was long ago. Gradually we became better off, and the emphasis changed. We started eating wild food—not out of desperation as we had done during the Great Depression of the early 1930s—but because of their fantastic and unexpected flavors.

My interest in cooking developed slowly at first; and it was the wild foods that sparked me on to try new recipes. I have divided this book into main sections by seasons, and within the seasons the arrangement is still phenological, so you can tell what you might expect to find when you go afield. (A few sections, e.g., mushrooms and fish, are treated as entire groups.) It is not a compendium of all wild foods, but an introduction to some of the tastiest in the Lake States. Every recipe has been tested in our farmhouse kitchen or in camp—most of them over and over again.

Madame Kuony of the Postillion School of Culinary Art—one of the most respected academies in the world—says, "Creation comes when you know the rules. First you must know the rules; then you can take liberties."

Please take liberties! Wild foods have been consumed since the dawn of man. Relatively speaking, wild food cookery is in its infancy. This book is based, not on inflexible recipes, but on the principles of dishing up gourmet food. If you always stick to the same recipe, and never vary it, each dish will taste just the way it did the last time you served it. "Just the same way" means it doesn't have a Chinaman's chance of tasting better than last time.

Some words of warning—

No matter how good it tastes, do *not* take a large helping of a species you have never eaten before. Just as some people get indigestion from lobsters and some are allergic to strawberries, you may encounter a species which is edible, and a treat for most people, but which does not happen to agree with you personally. This book does not cover toxicology—I suggest you consult other references on this subject.

Most of what I have written applies to the Lake States. If you are foraging outside this region, do consult local references.

In some ways the Indians had an easier life once upon a time than we do now. The complexities of county, state and federal regulations and laws are many. They change with such dizzying swiftness that all I can do is to advise you to keep up to date. There are, for example, places where one can get arrested catching frogs, and *paid* for shooting crows!

In general, wild animals are less contaminated than domestic ones. But some of our waters are so contaminated that their fish are safe to eat only in small quantities. Your local conservation officer can tell you about the best places to go fishing.

Some landowners object to having people traipsing over their property without permission. This is known as trespass.

Now I have warned you not to get sick, not to get in trouble with the law, and I have assiduously pointed out many little pitfalls along the way. Here is one more warning—and I hope you will take it seriously—don't ruin the flavor of any delicate recipe by overcooking!

Acknowledgments

Lots of people have helped with this book, including those who asked for second—or even third—helpings of my cooking. My special gratitude, however, goes to the late E. A. Benbrook, College of Veterinary Medicine, Iowa State University, who taught me so much about diseases of domestic animals and of wildlife;

to Margaret Guthrie, author of several highly successful cookbooks, who undertook the hideous task of conforming my wild food recipes;

to Ruth Louis Hine, a creative, stimulating editor who, with Frederick Hamerstrom, caused this book to come alive;

to George Knudsen, for twenty-five years State Naturalist of Wisconsin, who shares my love of the wilderness, but who sat indoors for many hours to critique my methods;

to William Silag of Iowa State University Press, who made getting edited fun as well as productive—and never once tried to make me a nicer person;

to Milton Trautman, who taught me how to cook fish, and who wrote the fish section for this book;

to Alexander Smith, author of many mushroom books, including *The Mushroom Hunter's Field Guide*. I followed him through woodlands learning mushrooms from him. He insisted that I keep collecting those dry, tiny mushrooms that nobody would think of eating, but in turn, he gave me his wife's excellent recipes for cooking delectable, succulent eating mushrooms;

and, most especially, I thank Frederick Hamerstrom who broke down one of my major prejudices. At sixteen, I declared, "I'll never cook for any man!" He manoeuvered me into changing my ways—it was Frederick who taught me how to cook.

SPRING

Spring is the season of green-up. After long
northern winters, our bodies crave greens. I
remember when we lived in the back country in
the 1930s, friends from the city asked, "What shall
we bring?" Our answer was greens. "Do bring us
spinach, fresh green peas. We don't crave meat
(we've had a-plenty) and we don't crave sweets. It's
greens we want."

Maple syrup

When spring is almost upon the countryside and nights are freezing but days are warm, maple sap is running. Perhaps snow is still deep in the woods, but if one waits too long one misses the big flow of sap.

Cut a few sumac stems about eight inches long and thumb-sized in diameter. Form troughs for the sap to run in by slicing off enough of each stem so that it is easy to scoop out the pulp.

Choose a drill that will ensure a snug fit for the sumac trough, and drill a hole in the tree about three or four feet from the ground. Push the trough into the tree, hang up your bucket to catch the drip, and listen for the sweet tinkle of the beginning of the sap run in your sugar bush. For a family of four, we tap ten trees.

Five-gallon plastic pails make excellent sap buckets. During a good run, one has to empty the buckets about every couple of days. Either cook down the sap in a big cauldron out in the woods, or boil it on the stove in a dishpan (a wide evaporating surface is an advantage). Thirty quarts of sugar maple sap make one quart of syrup. For soft maple, use a forty-to-one ratio. Syrup which has not been cooked down enough is apt to spoil.

The Indians are said to have used not only sugar maple, but also red maple, silver maple, and even box elder.

Cowslip (marsh marigold)

Cowslips should be gathered soon after the ice is out of the marshes and before they are in bloom. It is usually the appearance of the first yellow blossoms in the marshes or on the stream bank that remind us that cowslip time is almost over. The last chance to gather cowslips for greens is when the very first blossoms appear, for in a few days after they have started blooming, the mellowness of their flavor is gone.

It is curious how some plants get a reputation for being inedible. In Britain the marsh marigold has the reputation of being dangerously poisonous and is shunned. The story is told of an American botanist who gathered himself a nice mess of these greens in England. He cooked them and, despite the horrified protests of his friends—ate them. He suffered no ill effects.

This plant should be boiled, not eaten raw.

MARSH MARIGOLDS

Leaves, buds and stems
Vinegar or lemon juice
Salt

Boil the greens about 12 minutes in salted water. Season with a dash of vinegar or lemon juice.

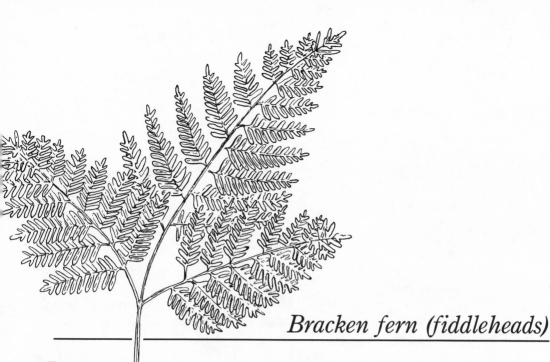

Bracken fern (fiddleheads)

When the flocks of geese have flown over and danger of frost is almost past, it is time to look for fiddleheads.

They tend to grow where there is white birch, aspen, or scrub oak and sometimes on maple soils. Often they are one of the dominant ground cover plants in young woods, and they may invade pastures and meadows in abundance. And now, a footnote of caution: The older fronds in particular are said to be carcinogenic. I believe they poison cows.

Jack Hausotter, a wild food expert, wrote me that in 1805–06, the historic Lewis and Clark expedition reported that Indians dug the roots of the bracken fern, and roasted them for food; and in 1976 one of his students, a woman from Korea, had makeshift tables across one side of her yard. There must have been nearly 200 square feet of surface covered with the shoots of bracken fern. She told him that in Korea, bracken fern shoots were selling for a dollar a pound.

I have not tried drying bracken. I pick fiddleheads when the fronds are still unfurled and don't eat them very often.

FIDDLEHEADS

Uncurled fronds
Butter
Lemon
Salt

Cook like green peas, boiling in salted water till tender. Drain off water, butter lightly, and sprinkle with lemon juice.

Water cress

Water cress grows along banks of slow streams and in springs.

Its leaves make a pretty and edible garnish for meats, and are a crisp, pungent addition to a salad. But best of all are cress and bread and butter sandwiches.

It keeps well as long as its stems are in water, and one can hold it for a week or more on the kitchen window sill using it as needed.

The submerged leaves of water parsnips sometimes grow mixed among the beds of water cress, especially in springs. Water parsnips are not wholesome. Avoid them. Water parsnips have jaggedly toothed leaflets. The leaflets of water cress are not toothed.

WATER PARSNIPS (Poisonous)

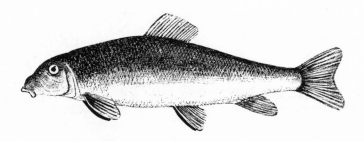

Suckers

In spring, when the pasque flowers are in bloom and the first early buttercups are appearing, the suckers begin to puddle. They come to the shallows to mate. It's time to catch them.

Boxing, netting, bow-hunting and spearing. For boxing, oldtimers used an old potato box—the kind with slats that can be plunged through the water quickly. I have watched an oldtimer standing in the water with hip boots on—standing, and staying perfectly still like an old heron. When a sucker came by, *plop* and he had the box over him. Fish for supper! Puddling suckers are near the surface in shallow water and can be caught with a landing net, shot with a bow and arrow, or speared—even with a pitchfork. Suckers have roundish mouths, toothless jaws, and often fleshy lips.

It is undoubtedly easier for a beginner to spear a sucker than to understand the fishing regulations of most states. Telephoning the local conservation officer can save you a lot of trouble; getting arrested takes the joy out of a sunny afternoon splashing around in the shallows. In Wisconsin, for example, you may use a bow and arrow, or spear, but never at night or where trout are present. Potato boxes are illegal and even sitting on one while fishing might look suspicious.

SUCKER PATTIES
(Oswald Mattson)

The meat of suckers has an exceptionally fine flavor, but most people are discouraged by the many tiny bones. Just ignore these little bones when making patties.

Skin and clean the sucker. Cut the meat away from the major bones and run it through the meat grinder 3 or 4 times. Add about one-half as much cooked potato as fish meat and enough raw egg to hold the mixture together. Season with finely chopped or ground onions and salt and pepper to taste. Fry.

According to George Becker (1983), the flesh of the blue sucker is firm, flakey, and well flavored. There are other suckers that are also good eating. Suckers are not easily confused with any unpleasant fish, so I eat any sucker I'm lucky enough to catch.

Dandelions

They may have been gypsies or they may have been Italians, but I shall never forget the day of their coming, for it was the first time I was ever taken for a grownup and the first day I cooked a wild vegetable.

My baby brother and I were out in the garden. Suddenly the lawn was full of women and children wearing bright scarves and blouses and full skirts—even the little girls wore earrings. They talked quickly in a foreign language as they dug dandelions from the very lawn I was accustomed to play on, moving across it slowly with knife blades shining in the sunlight.

I was twelve years old. Taking my little brother's hand, I approached them cautiously to watch what they were doing. It was when I was still trying to phrase a polite question to open the conversation that one of the women turned to me. Shaking the earth from a dandelion plant, she held it up for my inspection before tossing it into her basket. "Good," she said, and then pointing at the baby with her knife blade, she asked, "Your son?"

Elva Paulson

I ran to tell the grownups, "They thought the baby was my son, and can we have dandelions for supper?"

"Oh, you shouldn't have spoken to them."

"But *can* we have dandelions for supper?"

"*May* we?"

"May we have dandelions for supper?"

"Not today, dear, perhaps some other day."

My father stepped outside the door and stood on the porch a moment. Though he made no motion, it was as if he had waved a magic wand dismissing them. They picked up their baskets and their babies and departed—never to return. Once more the lawn looked as it always had, except there were fewer dandelions.

My day was not over. I built a fire behind the lilac bushes, and boiled my dandelions in a tin can, and ate them all. They would have tasted better with salt.

The common dandelion, *Taraxacum officinale,* is a weed introduced from Europe. The Japanese consider the flowers so beautiful that they grow them in their gardens. We, on the other hand, grub them out of our lawns.

For eating, it pays to know when to dig them. Dandelions often live only two years. Those gathered in spring are frequently old and about to flower, set seed, and die. Few people know it, but dandelions are at their very best in fall when their leaf rosettes are storing food-stuffs—often for the only winter they will know. They are worth trying in spring, but remember: Autumn dandelions are sweetest.

DANDELION GREENS

Boil tender young greens in salted water.

DANDELION WITH SOUR CREAM
(Charlotte von Sivers)

1 tablespoon fat
1 tablespoon flour
Hot, salted water
Sour cream or yogurt
Dandelions

Steam for 5 minutes over low heat. Add 1 tablespoon fat and 1 tablespoon flour and enough hot, salted water to make a thick sauce. Add sour cream or yogurt to taste. Stop cooking and eat!

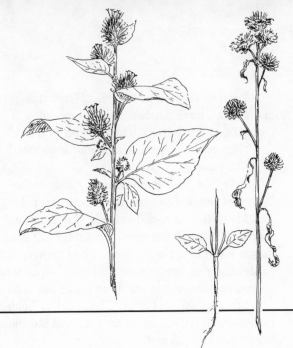

Burdock

The young leaves of burdock as a salad, or cooked like spinach, were recommended to me. One *can* eat them. A guest who tried them with us summed up the bitter flavor neatly. He put down his fork, looked out of the window for a moment, and then sighed, "Do you mind if I don't finish my greens?"

Stinging nettles

Nettles grow in waste places, often on peat soil. They can be annoying weeds and it is not unusual to find people trying to get rid of them by burning them. This is not only a waste of good peat, but it doesn't work since fire *encourages* nettle growth. If nettles are left unburned too long, other plants will crowd them out. If you want to keep your nettles, burn them from time to time, but never start the fire when the peat is dry. Remember that a patch six feet square should provide enough greens for the family.

NETTLE GREENS

Pick the plants when they are about a foot tall. Boil them for about 8 minutes. This not only cooks them, but also removes the sting. Cool enough so you can strip the leaves from the tough stems and serve the leaves with salted butter.

Or add raw nettle leaves, cut up fine, to soups. Boil 2 minutes.

Honey

I am not a real beekeeper. I like to catch bees, and to get them to go into a hive, where they make lots of honey for us and our friends. They would make more if I were a real beekeeper and kept track of the queen, and kept records of honey production.

It is strange that I have never tried to find bee trees and get my honey directly from the wild, the way both Indians and bears so soon learned to do after honey bees were introduced from Europe.

An oldtimer in New York State used to find his bee trees by taking an empty matchbox and putting a little flour in it. Next he'd catch a bee and put it in the box. After a few moments he'd let the bee go and follow it with his eyes — not too difficult as the bee was white with flour. He'd *mark the line* and follow it. Then he'd catch another bee and repeat the process until he was led directly to the bee tree.

Catching bees. If we don't catch our bees in May, we won't have honey in the fall. Early spring is the best time, but mid-spring is a more likely time to find a swarm. As the old saying goes,

> *A swarm of bees in May*
> *Is worth a load of hay.*
> *A swarm of bees in June*
> *Is worth a silver spoon.*
> *A swarm of bees in July*
> *Isn't worth a fly.*

We have always caught our own bees. Wherever it hangs, a swarm of bees is not only a challenge, but also looks like something that might go to waste. Of course any swarm might find itself a perfectly satisfactory abode, but we try to arrange it so the abode is one of our hives. I've caught and hived at least a dozen swarms, kept bees successfully for years, and had all the honey we could use or give away. My aim has not been commercial. For me, trying for maximum production would take all the fun out of bees. The very thought of buying bees is anathema to me.

Our family started out in the adventurous way. My brother, Putnam Flint, now a professional beekeeper, writes, "This is how I started before I knew any better. I used a sheet and a bushel basket propped up with a bit of 2 × 4 for an entrance. The bees went in one two three, and after dark I took the basket with bees and placed it behind my barn . . . Twenty-four hours later, I was amazed to find three beautifully spaced combs on the underside of the inside of the basket. I found the comb with the queen on it and placed it in the first bee-hive I ever built. As you know, the bees followed easy as pie."

Professional beekeepers presumably always have an extra hive ready; they, however, are apt to buy their bees, or have a pretty good idea when their own bees are likely to swarm. Our beekeeping has always been unpremeditated, and consequently we start making our preparations after we've found a swarm.

Bees can be hived into practically any box having approximately the right dimensions; however, even experienced beekeepers are often not keen about moving bees from makeshift equipment into a standard hive. *It pays to start with standard equipment.*

Beekeeping in Illinois by Elbert Jaycox (1969) is well worth owning if you think you might — just possibly — ever suddenly take up beekeeping. It has a particularly good description on how to build a standard hive.

Upon finding a swarm of bees, the first task is to size up the situation, so one will not be delayed by repeated trips for tools one *wishes* one had foreseen a need for. In any case, you will need an old sheet.

The bees must be dislodged. If the swarm is hanging on something solid, it will have to be scraped off (recommended tool: a long handled shovel). If it is hanging on something with a bit of flexibility like a rickety roof, or a medium-sized or small branch, the problem is easier. A stout blow with a mallet or axe jars them loose so the whole swarm falls.

If the swarm is high, consider: ladder, climbing irons, and plenty of rope. Possibly the swarm is high enough (over twenty feet or so) to warrant knocking them into a container, lest the bees disperse before landing on the sheet. In such a case bring along a wash tub and plan a way to have the bees fall directly into it. (One hives them later after one's brought them down.) Warning: a swarm of bees suddenly landing in a wash tub is *heavy*.

Having sized up the situation, we usually dash to a lumber yard, to a pile of boards, or to the nearest farm to knock together a hive. A bit of quick carpentry while the bees are still hanging on a tree saves one later handling when the bees are no longer swarming and when they have lost the unique gentleness characteristic of swarming bees.

One can hive bees alone, but it is far easier with two.

Buy, build, or borrow a hive. If it is near nightfall or cold or rainy, you will probably have hours, or possibly over a day to get this done before the swarm moves. In hot, clear daytime weather there is no predicting how soon it will move; one works as fast as one can.

To hive the bees. Spread an old sheet under the swarm. Place the hive near the highest corner of the sheet and arrange this corner so the bees may walk straight up onto the porch and into the hive. Jar the bees from their perch onto the sheet and let them walk into the hive.

Soon after they have fallen to the sheet, the sound of their humming changes to a mellower tone, and the majority will eventually start to move in one direction. If they select a direction other than the hive, move the hive so they will go into it. If you see the enormously large queen go into the hive, rest assured, the others will follow.

Selecting the permanent hive location. The hive should never be placed in deep shade. The entrance should face south. In the country, I would recommend placing the hive at least 100 yards from the house; however, bees may be kept on a rooftop in a city.

To move the bees. Return to your swarm after dark, by which time all the bees should be in the hive. Stuff the entrance shut with bits of screen and move the hive to its new location. This is a very simple operation, but after one's first day with bees, it gives one an eerie feeling to travel in a little automobile with a buzzing beehive. I consider it a weakness on my part, but I still prefer to use a truck and travel with bees in back – outdoors!

Place the hive in its new location and open the entrance. Pile a little brush or some weeds directly in front of the hive. The theory behind this is that when the bees come out the next morning, the brush calls their attention to a new situation. They will start circling, marking the location of their new home – instead of getting lost.

By this time one has probably discovered who the local authority on beekeeping is and can turn to him, or to a book for advice. Or call your county extension office.

If you have not been able to obtain frames, and your bees are simply in an empty box, they will start building combs in inconvenient convolutions. One saves not only work for oneself, but also the bees' valuable time, by installing movable frames promptly rather than waiting a week or so. Before the invention of movable frames it was the custom of primitive beekeepers to destroy the colony in order to get the honey.

Books on beekeeping usually have the professional in mind and mention many useful gadgets for quantity production. For two or three hives the following tools are sufficient:

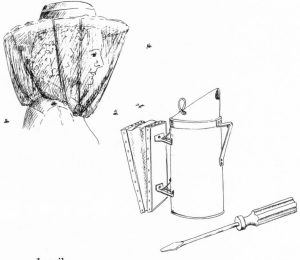

1 veil
1 large screw driver (for hive tool)
1 smoker, not too small. (Running out of smoke during a busy operation is a nuisance.)

The dry, dark red heads of sumac make a good and pleasant smoke.

Honey flows. One of the unexpected pleasures of starting beekeeping is learning the honey flows of one's own locality so that one can eat from the combs one likes best and give the rest back to the bees or sell it.

In Michigan, for example, the pale, mild, white clover honey has the highest commercial value, and it was not until we had our own bees that we tasted the aromatic basswood and tree flower honey of early spring, or the dark spanish needle and aster run of autumn which we found best of all.

Some of the important honey plants are alfalfa, sage, mesquite, buckwheat, fireweed (*Epilobium* sp.), raspberry, and sumac.

Honey may often be substituted for sugar in cooking, and for some types of cooking it is better.

Violets

When I was a freshman, one evening my date handed me the first violet of spring. I looked at it, told him its Latin name and then I ate it. It was our last date.

As a child I had lived in Europe for a time and remembered opening boxes of expensive chocolates. Sometimes the top tray was sprinkled with crystallized violets.

All violets are good to eat. Blue violets are the most decorative when crystallized. Pansies are even prettier, but not quite as tasty.

Violets grow in the woods, in meadows, and on high, dry ledges. It is a reflection on some of us that they often grow in ravines among old tin cans, bleach bottles, and rotting tires. I prefer to gather my violets far from rubbish and dumps.

CRYSTALLIZED VIOLETS

Egg white
Granulated sugar

Preheat oven (250°). Beat 1 or 2 egg whites until stiff. Dip each violet in the beaten egg white, then roll each flower in granulated sugar. Put them on waxed paper in an oven at 250° until they are dry (about 10 to 15 minutes).

Frogs

My first frogs were caught with a landing net near home, and then I went to visit the Austin Whites in Massachusetts. Their children, like other New England children, used to go frog hunting with BB guns, and were allowed to take the rowboat and row to an island with a pagoda.

We started frogging as soon as it was dark enough, with one to row the boat or hold the flashlight and the other to shoot or catch frogs. Usually as soon as we had a frog apiece, we built a small fire in front of the pagoda, skinned our frogs and roasted frog legs on sticks. We cooked them quickly, for we knew that at any moment someone from the big house on the hill would start calling, "Bedtime."

In those days frog legs were not commonly eaten in this country. Fishes, raccoons, and herons ate them and it was said that Frenchmen did too.

Not only the legs of bullfrogs, but also those of other frogs are good too.

LEOPARD FROG   WOOD FROG   BULLFROG   GREEN FROG

FROG LEGS

To kill frogs, break the backbone just back of the head. To prepare them for the table, cut off the head just back of the forelegs, skin and clean them and sauté quickly in butter. (The cook is entitled to all the little bits of back.) Serve the legs hot on thin slices of hot buttered toast.

Or if the fisherman of the family has caught something not quite big enough for a meal, garnish the fish with frog legs and serve with butter or tartar sauce.

KING'S INN FROG'S LEGS
(Faye and Randy Ware)

1 egg
½ can (5 ounces) evaporated milk
Salt and pepper
Flour
5 frog's legs
Fat for deep fat frying

Faye Ware and her son Randy of King's Inn *both* gave me this recipe. Randy started out by saying, "All we do is make a wash. . . ."

Convinced that I had misunderstood, I asked. "A *what?*"

"A wash," he repeated, "with egg, salt, pepper, and canned evaporated milk cut half and half with water."

"Why isn't that a batter?"

"Too thin to be a batter." Mrs. Ware added, "Then you dip the legs in flour and fry them."

"In deep fat?" I asked.

"Yes, two to three minutes in deep fat."

Last evening we ate at King's Inn. We drove 34 miles to the Texas coast to Loyola Beach for dinner, but people travel clear from Corpus Christi, Brownsville, or even from Laredo (124 miles one way).

As my rule is to test every recipe, I ordered one raw frog leg. The young waiter looked distinctly uneasy. Mrs. Ware kindly came to my rescue, and that poor young man brought me one large, skinned, raw frog leg in a ziplock bag. He saw me pop this trophy into my purse.

Today I cooked that single leg in King's Inn wash, and begin to understand why some people travel over 100 miles just for a meal.

Strawberries

On undisturbed meadows and in openings in the woods, wild strawberries start to set fruit at the time the ruffed grouse are hatching— roughly mid-June in the Lake States.

Of course, wild strawberries are good plain, with sugar, with cream, and for cooked jam. Fresh jam is not for keeping but for immediate consumption in camp.

FRESH STRAWBERRY JAM

Wild strawberries
Sugar

Crush the berries with enough sugar. Sweeten to taste. Spread on bread and eat. Or fill a pie shell and top with whipped cream.

The crushed, sugared berries keep beautifully in a freezer.

Snapping turtle

Snapping turtles occur east of the Rockies and are the largest inland turtles of the United States. Record turtles weigh up to 50 pounds, but 10 to 15 pounders are more commonly found.

They may be identified by the relatively small, roughly cross-shaped plastron or undershell and by the tubercles along the top of the tail.

They bite hard and if teased their attack is sudden and tenacious. To pick up a snapper, seize it by the tail and hold it from you. We have ordinarily caught ours on dry land. Rendall Rhoades (1950) describes underwater catching as follows:

The accepted method of catching turtles in streams is "noodling." A noodler goes along the bank of the creek and runs his arm back into the muskrat holes and root tangles for these are the favorite haunts of the big snappers. As he touches the turtle, he feels the shell carefully to determine the head end and the tail end and the turtle is removed by the tail. If the noodler pulls out a water snake, a half-grown muskrat or a hell-bender, that's all in a day's work and he goes on to the next hole in search of a turtle. This method is very productive.

Some may criticize me for describing how to kill a turtle. I have seen enough clumsy, slow attempts to deem it my duty to describe two swift, practical methods.

George Knudsen, for twenty-five years State Naturalist of Wisconsin, recommends picking the turtle up by the tail. This causes the turtle to stick out its head making it a relatively simple matter to hit it hard on the head with a heavy stick or a short steel bar. Knudsen is 6′3″ and one of the more powerfully built men it has been my pleasure to go afield with. Snapping turtles can weigh up to 50 pounds and not everyone is strong enough to lift a big turtle with one hand and deal a hard blow with the other.

This is the method I use on larger turtles: To kill a snapper quickly and efficiently, get it to bite the open jaws of a pair of pliers. In a trice you have the snapper's mouth and it has your pliers. It takes but a moment to cut its head off neatly. Novices hack away with a club or an axe, often failing to make a quick clean kill. If the turtle is so strong that you can't keep its neck extended, call a helper to hold the turtle while you hang onto the pliers with one hand and sever the head with the other.

Frank Renn and I learned from each other. I taught him how to kill a snapper quickly and besides not to waste neck meat by chopping away with an axe for decapitation. He taught me another lesson; how to utilize every morsel of meat from the rest of the turtle.

DRESSING OUT A TURTLE
(Frank B. Renn)

Scrub the decapitated turtle with laundry soap and a stiff brush until it is clean . . . and get a container of water, big enough to hold the turtle, boiling. When you have scrubbed off the leeches and green growths, boil the whole turtle for 30 or 40 minutes.

I like to work outdoors, so I take the turtle pot and dump it outside on the grass and leave it until the turtle is cool enough to handle. I turn it upside down and cut out the under shell. Again I let it cool.

There are seven different flavors of turtle meat. Some of the choicest lie along the backbone and it is almost hopeless to get this out if the turtle has not been boiled first. Now is the time to work with two dishpans. I toss the good meat into one and the discards into the other. When in doubt, I taste.

Muscle meat tends to be good, fat is often of low quality, and seek the liver carefully. It is often excellent, but the gall bladder must be cut away and discarded or its acrid taste will permeate, and your friends will wish that you had never come upon a turtle.

Snapping turtles are not only abundant, but also an epicurean delight.

FRIED TURTLE

Fry like chicken or pheasant.

TURTLE SOUP

Cook slowly, simmering over low heat with onions and a little salt. Some include the small intestines in turtle soup. Meat stock or bouillon may be added. Taste the soup when the meat is tender. Now is the time to decide whether to make plain turtle soup seasoned with sherry, or whether to add tomatoes, carrots, celery, etc.

Asparagus

Some people seem to have an uncanny ability to find the plump, inconspicuous shoots of early asparagus. Their magic method is to just look for last year's long-dead stalks. The first tender green sprouts will peep forth from the same roots. Some plants have massive root systems and a single plant often produces up to a dozen stalks for *one* picking.

Competition for roadside asparagus has become fierce. I know one gatherer who painstakingly hid "his" plants by cutting off all last year's stalks and carrying them away. He tied small wire markers on the fence near each plant—markers for his personal use. When he returned, hoping to gather asparagus, he found that every one of his little, secret markers had been removed!

BOILED ASPARAGUS

Raw asparagus has a pleasant flavor, but I prefer to boil this vegetable in salted water for 8 to 12 minutes.

SUPPER DISH OF SPRINGTIME

6 eggs (eggs are cheap in spring)
6 handfuls fresh-picked asparagus stalks
3 tablespoons shortening (butter or chicken fat)
3 tablespoons flour
1 chicken bouillon cube
About a cup of milk

Boil the eggs 12 minutes and then put them into cold water. Trim off the delicate asparagus tips and set them aside. Cut the asparagus into 1-inch lengths, and boil them 10 minutes. Ten minutes gives you plenty of time to make a white sauce. Heat the shortening; add the bouillon cube and flour. Cook three minutes, and then add milk slowly. Now put the cooked asparagus stalks into a serving dish, peel and slice the eggs and add them to the asparagus. Stir the sauce into this combination. Garnish with the delicate asparagus tips that you set aside. Serve immediately.

Mustard

Mustard greens are commonly gathered just before the plants push forth their yellow flowers. Cooked like spinach, they are a good pot herb. Black mustard and white mustard both have a pleasant taste and are common in weedy places. More recently mustards have taken over whole fields. As far as I know, they are not harvested in the United States and are still deemed weeds!

In Europe, however, these are the cultivated mustards. Black mustard is the principal source of table mustard, and white mustard is not only a source of table mustard—it is tasty as a salad as well. Mustard seeds are ground to supply our supermarkets.

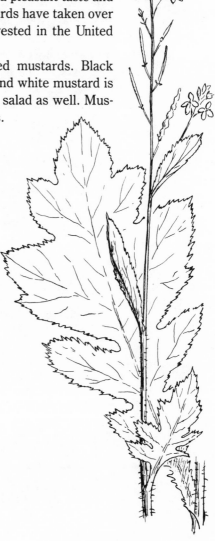

Common elder

When we visited our friend, Brigitte, she most commonly talked about opera, museums, and art, but sometimes we got onto subjects where our ignorance didn't show quite so much. I could hold my own talking about food. She is a superb cook and scorns the idea that baronesses should have their cooking done for them.

"Brigitte," I said one day as we were sitting together on a window seat, watching storm clouds build up against the sunset. "We ate something extraordinarily good in a little railroad restaurant. It was made of flowers—and later there are berries that turn dark."

I had gotten used to having my hostess unexpected and impulsive, but I was not prepared for her reaction this time.

"Rush, Fran, the elders are in bloom; we must hurry and pick some quickly before it rains."

She seized two big baskets and we did rush across a meadow to a swale where fragrant white blossoms grew on bushes. "Pick a great many, *pick*. If it rains before we finish, everything will be spoiled."

It was so that I learned a treasured recipe.

ELDER BLOSSOM FRITTERS
(Bavarian: Hollerkücherl)
(Baroness Brigitte von Fraunberg-Ebner)

25 elder blossom heads
3 eggs
1 cup flour (or less)
1 teaspoon oil
½ teaspoon salt
½ cup milk
Fat for deep frying
Sugar

Gather the flowers when they are fragrant
and in full bloom. Separate eggs. Mix egg
yolks, flour, oil, and salt. Add milk. Beat egg
whites into the dough. Leaving fairly long
stems on the flowers, dip them in the dough,
and fry slowly in deep fat. Test fat by dropping a bit of dough in, dough should turn
brown. Sprinkle with sugar and serve hot.
Eat blossoms, stems and all. (Serves 5.)

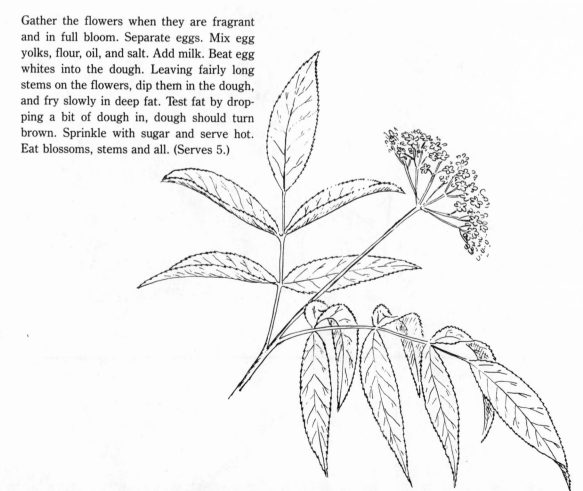

SUMMER

Man is an omnivore—people's teeth give them away. Anybody who has studied comparative anatomy knows that people teeth are not made for vegetables alone, nor just for meats. They are made for both.

Summer is a transition season. The acute hunger for greens is past, and my body (at least) craves a mixed diet—both meat and vegetables . . . and fish.

Fish from different waters, and from different times of year, do have different flavors. I have placed the fish section in early summer to give fish cookery a good start.

FISH

Experts on fish often haven't the slightest interest in eating fish; all too often they are content to munch peanut butter sandwiches and talk about fish. Dr. Milton Trautman, a scholar and an epicure, kindly wrote these instructions.

General instructions for fish

FREEZING

To prepare fish for the deep freeze we:

1. Catch them.

2. Throw them in the bottom of the boat or pack in ferns or grass and keep in a creel or shaded place where they remain alive or die out of water. (Nothing is more sorry than a dead, drowned, water-soaked, bacteria-laden fish that has been hanging on a stringer all day.)

3. Scale fish as soon as possible after catching (if catfish, skin them) and don't be particular about getting *all* the scales off.

4. Cut open the belly and remove the viscera (no need to take out the peritoneum). Do not remove any fins, except to take off the pelvics. Usually the cut along the belly, and where the head was attached, is the only exposed flesh. Exposed flesh causes the meat to dry out and offers opportunity for bacterial action.

The mucus on the fish has antiseptic qualities so do not rub it all off. Avoid putting the fish in water. The water in which fish are usually cleaned has some bacteria and any bacteria already on the fish will develop faster if the fish is washed.

But bacteria are not the main reason for not washing! The main reason is flavor. Loose muscle of fish flesh absorbs water rapidly, especially if the fish is filleted (a truly horrible practice for fresh, delicately flavored fish). [In my squirrel studies I take a 17 ounce gray squirrel and clean it. The carcass ready to eat weighs 8 ounces. If I place the carcass in a mild solution of salt water for ½ hour it weighs up to three ounces more, having absorbed as much water as that.] Then, when the fish is frozen, the muscle fibers are torn so the fish will be flabby when thawed. When fried, the water is driven out, the cooking fats enter, and you have the taste of fried grease, not the natural taste of fish.

PREPARING FROZEN FISH FOR COOKING

5. Cut or pull off the heads unless the fish is to be baked, in which case leave the heads on, removing only the eyes.

6. Run your hands along the side of the fish to remove lingering scales, or roughly brush it with a clean, dry rag.

7. Put enough fish in a pile for a meal and wrap tightly with freezer paper; label (e.g., 6 *Micropterus dolomieui* June 1975).

All of this seems sloppy and unorthodox, and bothers the average person because we use no water. But if you have really good taste buds, follow my advice.

THAWING

When we want fish to eat, we take a package from the freezer and allow the fish to thaw. While the fish are still quite cold we finally—this one time—place them in water, thoroughly clean away all the scales, mucous, and blood, and remove the peritoneum. We then lay the fish on paper towels to dry.

FRYING

Fish should be prepared for frying so that only the belly incision and where the head was can soak up grease; all the rest is protected by unbroken skin. Whenever possible we use only the smaller fish for frying. We never remove the fins because that allows the grease to enter; if the fins are quite large we cut them off near the base to allow for more frying space.

BROILING

Split fish in half, sprinkle with paprika and salt on the flesh side, and broil.

BAKING

A baked fish may or may not have a strip of bacon on it, and may or may not have a fresh sage-bread dressing.

What we have in all three methods of cooking is the natural flavor of fresh fish, each species with its most distinct flavor.

This distinctive flavor actually is not what the average American wants. Most Americans have eaten stale fish and do not like them. They have never had the opportunity to acquire a taste for the many distinctive-tasting fresh fishes. Now, one reason why fishes are filleted is because they are too stale, too soft, or too strongly flavored to eat in the round. By filleting a stale, strongly flavored or soft fish, and soaking it well in water, all fish and stale flavors are removed, and the fried product tastes like brown paper, heavily greased and salted.

Few flavors are more ephemeral than those of fresh fish. Even fishes properly cleaned and left in the freezer four months lose much of their best flavor although they are still very good. In fact a fish left in the refrigerator two hours loses a surprising amount of its flavor. To obtain the best in fishes, one must clean a freshly killed fish and immediately cook it.

There is considerable difference between the flavor of the same species of fish at different seasons of the year. Most freshwater species are much better flavored in August, September, and October than in early spring (which is against popular opinion that fishes from cold water are the best). Catfishes are an exception; they are best in June or July before they have begun laying up too much fat for the winter hibernation period.—Milton Trautman.

Fish recipes

It sometimes comes to pass that fish have been kept in the locker rather too long, or that one has caught fish that are not in prime eating condition. I am not talking about spoiled fish, which of course should be thrown away and not given to the cat, but simply about fish which for one reason or another are perfectly edible but no treat.

Cooked simply, these can never become a treat. Not every fish is destined to have its ephemeral essence preserved; some should become mere vehicles for spices and sauces.

In general, onions, cheese, tomatoes, garlic, pork fat, or potatoes are the backbone of many excellent fish dishes. For such, the cook, not the fish, should receive the praise.

The spontaneous evolution of regional recipes has been influenced not only by the native customs of the cooks, but also by climate and availability of first-rate fresh fish. In my opinion the best of the fancy fish recipes stem from the South, the best of the simpler chowders from the New England coast, and the best fish of all are fresh caught and simply cooked.

FLAKED FISH A LA CRÊME IN RAMEKINS
(Gowanloch 1933)

2 tablespoons of butter
1 tablespoon of flour
2 egg yolks
1 cupful of milk
2 cupfuls of boiled or fried fish flake (any fish will do)
1 teaspoonful of salt, a few drops of onion juice
1/8 teaspoon of paprika
1/4 cupful of buttered bread crumbs

Put the butter into a saucepan; when melted, remove from the fire and add the flour, stirring until smooth. Return to the fire and add the egg yolks and milk, which have been beaten together. Add slowly and stir constantly. When thick and smooth, add the seasoning and the fish. Fill the ramekins and cover with buttered crumbs. Place in a hot oven for a few minutes, or until the crumbs are a light brown. Garnish with parsley.

NEW ENGLAND FISH CHOWDER

4 pounds fish (cod, haddock, pollack, etc.)
1/4 pounds salt pork
4 onions
4 potatoes
3 cups milk (or 1 1/2 cups evaporated milk)
Salt and pepper

Boil fish until easily separated from bones. Discard bones. Fry cubed salt pork until there is fat enough in the pan to add and fry onions. Fry onions until brown. Add fish and sliced potatoes and the water the fish was cooked in. Cook until potatoes are done, if necessary adding more water. Add milk. Salt and pepper to taste, and serve with hardtack or common crackers.

Better still warmed up.

INLAND FISH CHOWDER

Cook as above, but add some salty, not oily, seafood: for example, a can of shrimp. Suitable fish: carp, suckers, bass, crappies, etc.

Trout. Trout should be scaled and gutted. It is customary to serve trout with heads and tails on, unless they are to be split for cooking.

FRIED TROUT

Fry small trout to golden brown using either butter or a shortening with a mild taste. Trout fried in mutton fat, for example, can be eaten, but the fine flavor of the trout is utterly destroyed.

BROILED TROUT

Broiled trout are excellent. Small trout need not be split before broiling. Serve with lemon slices, and garnish with small sprigs of wood sorrel or with large sprigs of water cress.

HUGO'S BAKED TROUT
(Dr. Hugo Schneiders)

Fry a large trout until browned. Then place it in the oven (300°), smothered in cream, salt lightly. The cream, bubbling slowly keeps the trout from drying out, and the combination of the browning and the cream makes this an epicurean dish.

Salmon. Poking about in the woods and marshes has a far greater appeal to me than going to garage sales. But, about 1973, I did go to a garage sale. I bought one item— a metal platter—and I bought it only because it had such a lovely shape and it reminded me of my father's pewter collection. I was ashamed of my purchase because I don't approve of buying objects for their beauty alone unless they are going to be hung on the wall. The platter cost 15 cents and it has become a treasured possession for baking, roasting, and serving fish and game—especially salmon.

BAKED SALMON WITH SHRIMP SAUCE

I bake other big fish like salmon.

4 thick slices of bacon, or salt pork
1 5-pound salmon, or ½ 10-pound salmon

Preheat oven to 350°. Arrange 4 thick slices of bacon, or salt pork, on a large oven-proof platter. Put the fish on these thick slices, so it won't stick to the platter. Cut some diagonal gashes along the upper side of the fish, and put a little bacon fat in each gash. Roast 45 minutes.

And for Shrimp Sauce:

3 tablespoons margarine or butter
3 tablespoons flour
Powdered shrimp bouillon to taste—mind you, no salt! Or pull apart a shrimp bouillon cube. Add piecemeal—*to taste.*

(Both shrimp bouillon products, "caldo de camarón," are put out by the Swiss company Knorr. The powdered bouillon, which comes in glass jars, is far superior, but we have only been able to buy it in Mexico. The bouillon cubes are beginning to appear in larger American supermarkets, sometimes near bouillons, and sometimes near Mexican foods. It is probably easier to catch a *big* salmon than to shop for shrimp bouillon.)

SHRIMP SAUCE OMELETTE

If possible, make some extra shrimp sauce. Put it in the refrigerator, and then—for breakfast—heat 1 cup of sauce, whisk in 8 eggs, and cook very slowly in a buttered frying pan. Turn when not quite dry: a most delicious omelette.

FLAKED SALMON

And, if there is left-over salmon, take out the bones and flake the meat. Add shrimp sauce to cover and heat up this pleasant luncheon dish. Nice served with boiled milkweed pods.

WHITEFISH
(Milton Trautman)

To prepare one of our greatest gastronomic treats we go aboard a fishing boat when she docks late in November, and carries hundreds of pounds of whitefishes (not white bass). We carefully paw the available males (males are readily identified; they have small tubercles on their body scales) and pick out a plump, live, three-pound fish (never a female; they are often poorly flavored). Hurry home, clean and split it, cutting it into about one pound slabs. Salt and cover cut parts with paprika (paprika makes the flesh toast brown). If the fish is very fat, turn skin side first to the fire, letting just enough fat drain out, then turn and sear the flesh side. If the fish is not too fat, turn the flesh side first to the fire, then when the slab is turned over the fats are sealed in the fish. Frequent turning seems to make the fats migrate from one side to the other, improving the flavor. Serve with coffee, bread and butter, and salad.

Roe. It is often a pleasure to watch fishermen clean their catch. Many work with sharp knives and skillful fingers. My pleasure in this performance is often dimmed by watching them throw away the roe to feed the bass, the dogs or the cats. I've obtained some first rate meals by simply offering to clean fish for people who didn't like the job and who could not be persuaded that fish eggs (roe) are delicious.

Not everyone is so unappreciative. A Wisconsin fisherman named Junior was startled by an unexpected scene aboard a chartered boat in Oregon. One of the group wanted to keep the eggs of his fish and angrily claimed they belonged to him. The captain—equally angry—pointed out that the eggs belong to "the boat." The fisherman just got the fish.

Salt water fishermen have been known to throw the flesh of the rather boney shad away and save only the roe for the dinner table!

Dr. Milton Trautman says there is as much range in flavor of fresh water fish eggs as in the fishes themselves. The bright green eggs of the gars are poisonous; the eggs of the dogfish may be poisonous as well. Most of us catch other species.

The eggs of smelt, bluegills, sunfish, black bass and of calico bass are especially delectable. Those of carp, carpsuckers and some other species don't always taste good. But Henry Smith states (n.d.), "The best part of the carp is the roe." Try it. Who knows at what time of year and under what conditions it is tasty?

Imported caviar costs $28.00 an *ounce*. It is an internationally famous delicacy. And what does it consist of? Salted roe of sturgeon and certain other large fishes! But I've salted the eggs of smaller fishes too— stirring in 2 to 6 percent of salt (by weight). Taste it and then try to store it in the freezer until company comes.

Hamlet says of a play, " 'Twas caviare to the general," i.e., above the taste of the common people. But then, Shakespeare may never have wanted gamefish roe, spread thin on a Ritz cracker and seasoned with just a drop of lemon juice.

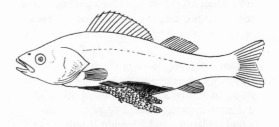

Fresh roe is the best of all, but when one has finished pulling out the little "bags" of eggs from a day's catch, the quantity may amount to less than a teacup. Wrap them up and put them in the freezer until you have enough for a meal. Don't wash them. Not only will you lose flavor, but bacteria will develop faster as a result of washing. Leave any washing you feel impelled to do until after you have thawed them.

FRIED ROE

Sauté slowly and serve with or without fish.

SCRAMBLED EGGS OF HENS AND FISHES

Using a small amount of butter or bacon fat,
sauté the roe, breaking it up into little pieces
while cooking. When nicely browned, add
hens' eggs and salt. Finish cooking over low
heat.

Fish liver. Fish liver sometimes tastes very
good fried like roe.

   The Indians believed that the livers of
lake trout were sometimes poisonous.
However, this is probably a myth. Mary
Phillips, epicurean chef of Bayfield's Old
Rittenhouse Inn in Wisconsin may be the
only chef *anywhere* to cook with lake trout
livers. She said to Tom Davis the columnist,
"The fishermen told me they were toxic.
They'd always thrown them to the gulls."
Phillips considers them even better than
whitefish livers.

Lamb's quarters

Lamb's quarters are also called "pigweed," and in Quebec "Poulette
grasse" or "Chou gras."

   A "weed" has been defined as "a plant out of place." I am inclined
to agree with the botanist who wrote, "The gardener, industriously
rooting out the pigweeds to admit air and sunshine to his spinach rows,
destroys, perhaps, the better plant . . . "

   Likely places to find pigweed or lamb's quarters are neglected
gardens and around barnyards.

   Boil in salted water like spinach. One eats the leaves and flowers,
stripping them away from the rather tough stems.

   Cattle graze certain parts of a pasture and neglect others. They
graze again and again in the same areas where growth is fresh and
new. I follow the same pattern when picking lamb's quarters. The
growth will be fresh and new and tender for the pot where I've picked
before.

   Lamb's quarters are also excellent in tossed salads with light vinai-
grette.

Crayfish

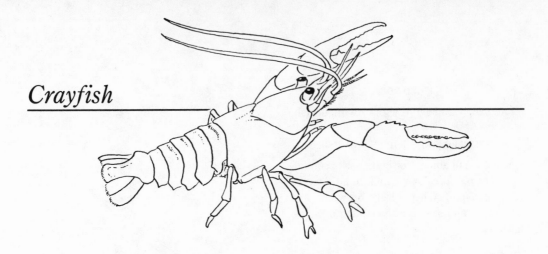

Crayfish, which look like little lobsters, inhabit the quiet waters of slow streams, lake shallows, and swamps. Sometimes they are called "crawfish" or even "crawdads." One species, the chimney crayfish, makes underground water-filled burrows with mud turrets several inches high at the openings.

We fish for them in the water. They lurk under old boats, under old boards and among the waterweeds—especially among the mats of Chara, or they may hide in tin cans and under stones or bury themselves in the mud. As soon as they are disturbed, they take off with astonishing speed swimming backwards and fast, and usually head straight for deep water. It is convenient to know which direction they are going to take.

One can usually get them with a landing net, but not nearly as many will get away if one uses a stout crab net with a four-foot handle. After dark, one can sneak up on them, shining them with a flashlight, and often catch them barehanded.

Occasionally they come up out of the water and wander around on the beach at night. Harry Walker, who used to be our postmaster, has told us of catching them by the bucketful on a small lake shore at ten o'clock at night.

We have always had to get ours the hard way: rolling logs and stones and then splashing through water in full pursuit. It is well worth it. Fifty crayfish make a nice portion, and a half-bushel bag serves five or six.

HOW TO PREPARE

Season the water in which you are about to boil the crayfish with plenty of salt, black pepper, and red pepper too. Then bring the water to a boil in a big pot. Add the crayfish and bring the water to a boil again and boil for 5 minutes with the pot uncovered. Cover the pot and let the crayfish set for another 5 minutes.

Drain off the water as soon as they have set, and when they are cool enough to handle, husk out the tail meat. Break the shell of the crayfish near the last pair of legs and try to pull the shell off the legs in one piece. With a little practice it's about as quick as shelling peas.

CRAYFISH SALAD

Chill the tailmeats and add them to a bowlful of lettuce which has been thoroughly dried, and torn into small pieces.

Stir in a good supply of French or Russian dressing to which a dash of tabasco has been added. Serve immediately.

BAKED-CREAMED CRAWFISH
(Gowanloch 1933)

2 tablespoons butter
1 tablespoon flour
2 cups cream
1 teaspoon onion, chopped fine
½ teaspoon parsley, chopped fine
1 tablespoon lemon juice
1 quart cooked and picked crawfish
Butter, salt and pepper to taste

Make a white sauce of butter, flour, cream, seasonings; add fish. Cook five minutes. Put into shells or ramekins; cover with buttered crumbs. Place in oven and bake 10 to 20 minutes until crumbs are brown. This may be used on toasted crackers or plain toast by increasing the amount of cream used, making the mixture thin enough to be poured over the toast. Garnish with parsley and lemon.

Margaret Guthrie suggests that I add, "Make a roux of flour and butter, cook over medium heat for 3 to 4 minutes. Add cream gradually, stirring constantly to avoid lumping. (If sauce lumps, strain it.) Add spices, then fish . . . ."

Crow

In some states crows may be killed whenever they are doing damage, or about to do damage. Crows doing damage are often eating corn and this should make them taste particularly good.

LARDED BREAST OF CROW

Skin the crow and cut off the breast meat. Place in dripping pan, covered with thin slices of salt pork, and bake about 25 minutes at 375°. In the meantime, boil the legs, back, liver, and heart for gravy stock, or for soup.

Summer salads

Sometimes when one has left a beautifully tended garden for three or four weeks, one comes home to a horrid surprise; *the weeds have taken over.* Instead of thrifty rows of peas, spinach, lettuce, and corn, one finds pusley, mallow, sheep sorrel, wood sorrel, and lamb's quarters — all excellent salad plants.

Salads taste curiously flat without dressing. If one is eating salad weeds for fun or to stretch the budget, conventional salad dressings improve the taste of wild salads or of lettuce mixed with weeds. The Indians used to put salad leaves on ant hills and let the ants run over them as a substitute for vinegar. Shake the ants off before eating such salads.

Mallow. Mallow often comes up in the pansy bed. The little "cheeses" — the fruiting mallow heads — have a fine flavor raw, and gathering them can keep little fingers busy for a long time.

Pusley. These low, fleshy herbs tend to become abundant in untended gardens when summer is well advanced. The small, stemless, 5–6 petalled flowers open only on sunny mornings.

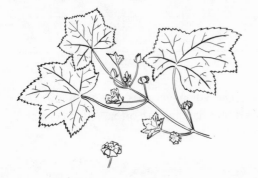

PUSLEY GREENS

Boil the above-ground parts of the plant, not long, but until wilted down. Serve with butter and either lemon or vinegar.

PUSLEY SALAD

Chop up the leaves and stems, and serve with oil and vinegar, or any thin salad dressing.

Sheep sorrel. Sheep sorrel grows in poor or abused soils and is often to be found in pastures. The leaves, chopped fine, give piquancy to a salad – and they are rather nice to nibble on.

The leaves are often discolored, but their flavor is good in spring, summer and autumn, whether they are green or have turned reddish.

During the drought of 1976 lawns turned sere, lilac leaves wilted and birch trees died, but sheep sorrel throve. It pushed out great over-sized leaves of extraordinarily fine flavor. This plant contains oxalic acid and should not be eaten to excess.

Wood sorrel. This delicate little herb is to be found in sunny situations, particularly where the soil has recently been disturbed, throughout the late spring and summer.

The flavor is tart, acid, and refreshing, and sprigs of wood sorrel are exquisite as a garnish for fish.

Small quantities taste very good in any sort of salad.

This plant should not be used as a vegetable or eaten in large quantities as it contains oxalic acid.

A sprig bearing 8 or 10 leaves and a few flowers per portion is sufficient for an attractive edible garnish.

Common milkweed

Common milkweed, unlike most weeds, has a long "eating season." The tender young shoots are first-rate; then the leaves are good as long as they still stay rather close to the stem and before they branch out and get tough. After that the flower buds emerge and they are tasty too. Best of all I like the pods when they are 1 to 1½ inches long. I'm not sure that they taste better than other parts of the plant but they certainly do mystify company . . . especially when found floating about in a plate of home-made chop suey. Cook in salted water until tender (about 10 minutes). Test from time to time by sampling a morsel.

Not all milkweeds are known to be wholesome; and some plants with milky juices are poisonous, for example:

Spurges (Euphorbiaceae) have a bad reputation as food. The leaves of spurges are scattered or alternate and not opposite like those of the milkweed.

Dogbane (Apocynaceae) should not be eaten. The leaves, like those of the milkweed, are opposite, but the plants are usually smooth and not slightly wooly like the common milkweed. Dogbane plants fork soon; those of the common milkweed do not.

Sometimes it is possible to find last year's seed pods to make identification easier. Dogbane has very slender seed pods. Some milkweeds also have rather slender seed pods, but common milkweed, which is such an excellent pot herb, has plump seed pods.

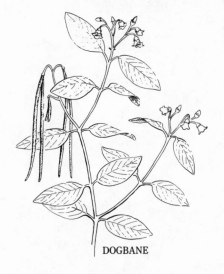

DOGBANE

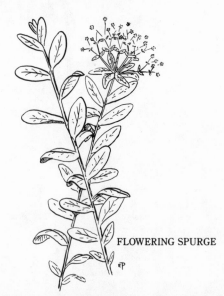

FLOWERING SPURGE

Woodchuck

The woodchuck, marmot, or groundhog—sometimes even called "whistle pig"—is really a squirrel.

It climbs trees badly, swims badly, and is usually not very far from its hole, into which it pops quickly. After a good fright, it is not very apt to come out again for ten or fifteen minutes. At first it will only show its head a few times. Unfortunately woodchucks are often lost by inexperienced hunters who cannot resist squeezing the trigger too soon. One should wait until it is well above ground and properly out of its hole.

Not infrequently woodchucks cause enough crop damage so that farmers class them as varmints.

TO PREPARE

Dress out immediately. Skinning may be put off for a few hours if need be. Look for and remove the glands beneath the "armpits." These may give the meat a strong taste.

FRIED WOODCHUCK

Select a young woodchuck. Cut into about ten pieces, roll in flour, salt, and fry like chicken.

WOODCHUCK STEW

1 big woodchuck
5 sprigs mint
1 large onion
½ teaspoon ground clove
1 bouillon cube
Salt and pepper

Put back and legs in pot. This is about all the edible meat a woodchuck provides. Cover with water. Add salt, pepper, mint, bouillon cube, clove, and sliced onion. Boil until water is almost gone. Remove bones and serve on toast.

These pretty little creatures are often considered pests, and are commonly called "gophers." They can be destructive in a garden.

To catch ground squirrels, pour water down their hole and stand ready to catch them as they emerge.

Drowning them out is simple with a garden hose, but very difficult without running water. (They do not drown, but pop out of the hole.) It pays to have them pop into a net, and be ready to hit them on the head quickly, for they can bite with unexpected severity. Another, somewhat simpler method is to set rat traps baited with peanut butter.

The meat is first rate. Fry slowly.

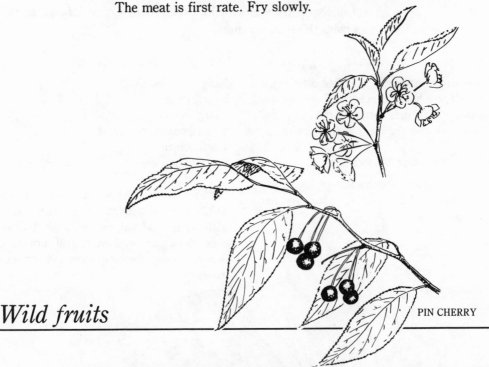

PIN CHERRY

Wild fruits

There are many kinds of wild plums and cherries, and from the eating standpoint their qualities are various. From some, it is easy to loosen the stone for jam and jelly making, some are good to eat raw, but many are tart and puckery.

Sometimes they grow on trees, but several species grow on such low and inconspicuous bushes that one could walk right through a patch without noticing fruit, for the picking is at shin height.

The flavor of wild cherries seems to vary little but wild plums are another matter. A single plum thicket may consist largely of trees bearing tart plums, a few trees with good eating plums, and one tree perhaps with exceptional plums – a tree to remember and come back to another year.

The insides of the stones and the wilting leaves of plums and cherries, both cultivated and wild, may contain prussic acid, a poison if eaten in large quantities.

The puckery wild cherries – chokecherry, pin cherry, and wild black cherry, for example – are particularly valuable in cooking. Their juices are a good substitute for lemon juice, and they are excellent combined with some of the abundant, but rather tasteless wild fruits, such as elderberries and juneberries.

One can gather quantities of wild cherries with ease if one waits until the ripe cherries are just ready to drop. Spread a large cloth or canvas on the ground to receive the crop and give the tree a good shaking.

Jam and jelly

We enjoy a campfire, and I tend to make jam in camp, which is usually near enough the car so that it's no trouble to take along extra sugar, some jars and, in case of need, some pectin.

If the fruit has stones, boil it (with as little water as possible) till it is soft enough to take out the stones easily. Very little water is needed as the fruit's own juices will supply part of the liquid needed to keep the bottom from burning; add more water if needed. Cool the fruit and dispose of the stones.

If your camping equipment, like ours, does not have kitchen scales, cut a straight stick and notch it at both ends and in the middle. Hang it up with a pot at each end: one with fruit and one with sugar. Add or subtract sugar till the pots balance. Combine the ingredients, cook and stir until thick. Keep tasting it. If too tart, add elderberries or juneberries. If too bland, add any of the wild cherries or even lemon juice.

WILD PLUM

If you don't have enough jam to make you happy, cook up some unripe wild grapes or green apples, which supply natural pectin (or use commercial pectin). Don't overcook your jam just because you want to add pectin; it would destroy the fine flavor of the fruit. (You can double the quantity and halve the flavor with pectin—some like it that way.)

Wild fruit jam is an epicurean delicacy and makes welcome presents.

Plums. Symbiosis—so to speak, a mutual benefit society between two creatures of different species—was at work this year. Something, I suspect a red squirrel, was ahead of me in the plum thicket. That creature wanted the *stones* and only ate enough of each plum to achieve its goal. I gathered the little cups of pitted fresh fruit—fully aware that my task of pitting would be less than usual.

Frozen jams need less cooking than preserves and retain the freshness of sun-ripened fruit. Frozen wild plum jam is superb served over vanilla ice cream and earns its place as well over slices of homemade bread.

FROZEN WILD PLUM JAM

4 pounds of wild plums
4 cups sugar
1½ cups water

Boil the plums with as little water as possible and only until their skins begin to pop. Cool the plums. I pour the juice off into one pot and set the other pot with the remainder into a basin of cold water. Being of an impatient nature, I start throwing away the stones as soon as I can do so without scorching my fingers. Once I have rid myself of the stones, I add sugar to taste, and bring the mixture to a boil for ½ minute. Plums vary in tartness and this year I added 4 cups of sugar to 4 pounds of plums.

PLUM PRESERVES

Follow the above recipe, but boil for about 5 minutes at the end instead of just bringing to a simmer. Frozen jam is better, but plum jam is a fine product too. It is darker, more easily transported, and keeps its flavor at least six years.

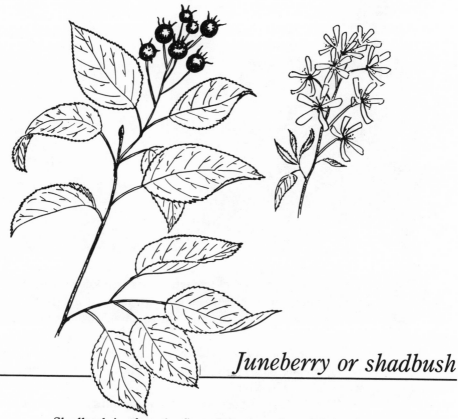

Juneberry or shadbush

Shadbush is often the first of the conspicuous berry-bearing bushes to bloom in spring. In some species the blossoms appear before the leaves, and these, as it happens, are easily forced in a vase on a sunny window sill—not for fruit, but for the delight of having great sprays of flowers indoors in late winter. (The reason it's called 'shadbush' along the east coast is that the blossoming usually signals the run of shad up the rivers. Shad roe time!)

The fruits look rather like oversized blueberries, usually purplish or black, sometimes reddish, and rarely white. Each berry is divided into ten compartments, each of which contains one small seed.

The berries are sweet and good to eat, tasting somewhat like blueberries.

If they are cooked, they tend to taste too mild, unless, as is recommended for elderberries, juices of tarter fruits are added.

Raspberries and thimbleberries

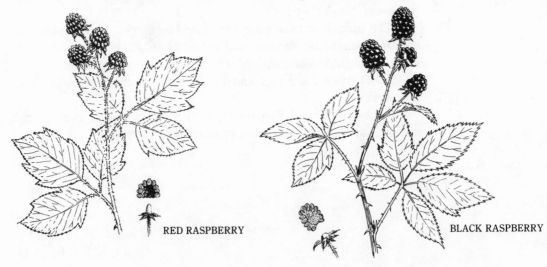

THIMBLEBERRY

Wild red raspberries seldom differ in taste from the cultivated ones which one buys in the grocery store. However, picking one's own red raspberries has a distinct advantage, for one knows their history and need not feel impelled to wash them. Washing raspberries destroys the delicate bloom on the fruit and causes an appreciable deterioration in flavor.

Although most of the red raspberry crop may fail in dry years, the plants growing near water along ditch banks and stream edges may bear well in spite of drought.

Thimbleberries and black raspberries are easily separated from the receptacle. In other words, they come off the plant like little caps. They are common around abandoned farms, open woods and thickets.

Both raspberries and thimbleberries have shield-shaped bugs about a half an inch long sitting on some of the berries. These bugs often leave an unpleasant taste on the berry. Don't just knock off the bug; throw away the berry the bug has been sitting on as well.

RED RASPBERRY

BLACK RASPBERRY

Elderberries

Elderberries have a mild, pleasant, but almost flat flavor. They are often easily gathered in great quantity. They are common, and the berries are free of cumbersome seeds. The heavy, flat-topped clusters of blue-black berries are a common sight along moist roadsides, and few of the clusters are so high as to be out of reach.

Whether used for jelly, pie filling or sauce, elderberries are a good base. By themselves, the taste is uninteresting; with the addition of sugar and juices of wild cherry, wild plum, or highbush cranberry, the culinary possibilities are many.

Blueberries

Carloads of people used to pour out of the cities after brush fires. Some raked the berries and dumped them into buckets, to sift out the green berries and leaves when they got home. At home, they threw the berries onto a screen just coarse enough so the ripe berries stayed on the screen, and the little green ones fell through the mesh. Next they turned on an electric fan and blew away the leaves and chaff. Most of what was left took little picking over.

Blueberry country is disappearing. The public does not realize what ecologists know: fire is natural. Wild fires can be disastrous to property, but controlled burns are necessary for many plants and animals. Someday—perhaps—Smokey Bear will become educated.

Blueberries grow thicker after a fire. They are delicious. Bears know this too.

Rose hips

Konrad and Gretl Lorenz came to visit us on their first trip to America. Gretl got up early and wandered about in the garden, and then, at breakfast, she exclaimed, "Your rose hips are so very fine." Suddenly I felt remiss. I had not even put a vase of flowers in the bedroom for her! It didn't take me long to cut a fine bouquet of rose hips. I planned to get it up to the room before she saw what I was carrying.

"Fran, where are you going with those?"

"To your bedroom."

"No, please *not!* We must make jelly."

And now, February 1988, I have just heard from Konrad. "The Rose Hip recipe awakens a number of very mixed memories, amongst others my collecting rose hips for the prisoners in a Russian camp to extract vitamins. But I prefer thinking of Gretl making jelly. . . ." Then came the postscript, "The recipe for the Rose Hip Jelly does not contain any information about how to separate the hairy seeds from the aromatic and vitamin-rich red shell." So I'd left something out. Fixed.

ROSE HIP JELLY
(*Gretl Lorenz*)

Boil equal parts of sugar and rose hips in enough water to keep from scorching. As soon as the hips are soft enough, mash them in this brew, and boil 5 minutes longer. *Pour the mixture into a nylon stocking and, as soon as it is cool enough, squeeze out the pulp and juice.* Sometimes one must add pectin to get a firm jelly. It tastes like apple jelly, but more delicate – which is not surprising because apples belong to the rose family. (If your jelly doesn't jell, you've made a fine drink.)

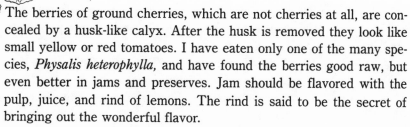

Ground cherries

The berries of ground cherries, which are not cherries at all, are concealed by a husk-like calyx. After the husk is removed they look like small yellow or red tomatoes. I have eaten only one of the many species, *Physalis heterophylla,* and have found the berries good raw, but even better in jams and preserves. Jam should be flavored with the pulp, juice, and rind of lemons. The rind is said to be the secret of bringing out the wonderful flavor.

Peterson's *A Field Guide to Edible Wild Plants of Eastern North America* (1977) lists four edible species. Tomatillo, one of the tantalizing ingredients in Mexican green sauce, salsa verde, is a ground cherry.

Mixed berries

Some people use red currants for jelly and jam. We find a far higher use as the essential ingredient in New England fruit pudding—a dessert of mixed berries.

NEW ENGLAND FRUIT PUDDING

1 quart red currants (these give the pudding its characteristic flavor). Do not substitute.
1 quart blackberries, thimbleberries, juneberries, or elderberries
1 quart blueberries or huckleberries
1 quart strawberries or raspberries
Dry bread
Sugar

Put a layer of broken dry bread in the bottom of a large bowl, cover generously with mixed berries (in the proportion of one part currants to three parts other berries). Sprinkle with sugar. Repeat this process until all the berries are used up. Poke with a potato masher to start the juices running. Chill for an hour or two before serving. May be served with heavy cream, or plain.

QUICK METHOD

Prepare as above, but mash each layer until the bread is saturated with berry juices. Serve as soon as no scrap of bread remains white.

The bread should be dry. It is a pity to waste good homemade bread in a pudding. Long ago bakeries sold big bags of old bread stuffed into 100-pound flour bags for 50 cents. By late summer of 1973 the price had risen to $2.00 a bag. It was still a bargain. Now, it is not available at all. At any rate, to keep the true flavor of New England fruit pudding, avoid "bakery sugar," cinnamon, and other distracting tastes. Sort out the plain white or whole wheat pieces for your pudding.

The best of the rest can go into any other bread pudding. The worst of the rest can go to the birds or the pigs.

Black nightshade

The black berries of this common weed have an odd, bland but rather pleasant taste. It is said that the berries are poisonous when green and unripe and that the poison is an alkaloid.

A. O. Stevens writes, "The plant has long been considered poisonous and contains solanine, but probably is not more injurious than potatoes or tomatoes. The berries are eaten in pie and preserves by many people . . . . The name 'deadly nightshade,' which is often applied to the black nightshade, is probably responsible for much of its ill repute. Deadly nightshade, *Atropa belladona,* is a European plant, not found in America. It has a very poisonous berry somewhat resembling the fruit of our species." It is said that nursemaids used to hang bunches of these poisonous berries over the cribs of fretful babies to make them stop crying and put them to sleep.

For my part, it never occurred to me to hang nightshade over my babies. (I did sometimes put a hat over their faces which often produced a salubrious effect similar to the hooding of my falcon!) I have eaten ripe black nightshade berries for years with pleasure, but would no more recommend the eating of *unripe* berries than the consumption of potato sprouts. Potato sprouts contain solanine – a poison.

Eat the ripe black berries raw. Do not eat the red berries of bittersweet nightshade (*Solanum dulcamara*).

Hog peanut

These beautiful little plants with their twining stems covered with brownish hairs grow in rich damp woodlands. They bear two and sometimes three kinds of flowers. The lower flowers develop into eminently edible subterranean fruits.

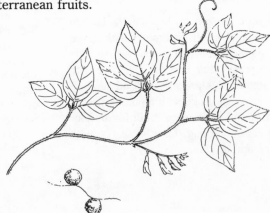

Fox snake

Last weekend my friend, Alan Beske, joined us in a turtle feast and today he brought us a three-foot, road-killed fox snake. His first thought was "No, no she wouldn't—not *Snake*—I'll just bring it in because it's so pretty. . . ."

He brought it in. "Fox snake! Do you want the skin?"

Alan did; he skinned and cleaned the snake. He offered to soak it in salt water, but I pointed out that would draw out the flavor.

We cut it into 3 inch lengths, floured it lightly and fried it in butter, till light brown (about 15–20 minutes).

Snake is best picked up by the fingers for eating. It is a delicacy to be savored as hors d'oevres, but to be served simply with saltines or potato chips.

Snake steak is easier to eat than fish, for the ribs stay attached to the backbone.

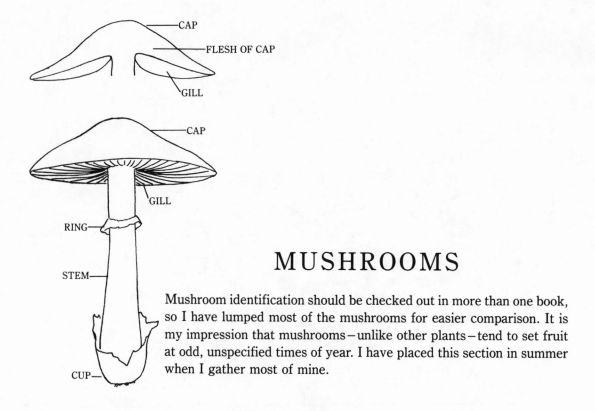

MUSHROOMS

Mushroom identification should be checked out in more than one book, so I have lumped most of the mushrooms for easier comparison. It is my impression that mushrooms—unlike other plants—tend to set fruit at odd, unspecified times of year. I have placed this section in summer when I gather most of mine.

Learn to know the mushrooms

To start eating mushrooms one should learn to know the species. The vinegar test, the silver coin test, etc., are worse than worthless for they give one a false sense of security and may get one poisoned. Also, just because something has nibbled a mushroom does not mean that it is safe. Squirrels, flies, and beetles can feast safely on mushrooms which may poison men, women, and children.

Don't try to take on the whole mushroom world at once. Select one to a few species and study them thoroughly, beginning by looking at the pictures. The underground part of the stem is sometimes important in identification. If possible bring home quite a few of one "kind" to have a good sample for study. Having checked the points in the written description, one can either throw away or send to an expert those which do not fit. When I'm learning a new mushroom, I don't let myself assume that it must be all right because it "almost fits". . . no matter how good its aroma, or how tempting it might look—delicately browned on a thin slice of crisp toast.

Gradually, with increasing experience, one notices that there is variability within each species. At first one is in no position to judge whether these variations are differences within the same species, or whether one has gathered more than one species. By the time one can recognize a typical specimen with the ease of a ten-year-old boy identifying a Cadillac, one has learned a good deal about variation.

Spore color is sometimes an important characteristic in species identification.

To make a spore print: break off the stem if any, and place the cap (gills down) so that it rests partly on white paper and partly on black. Cover with a glass.

After an hour or two, examine the color of the spore print that has formed under the mushroom. The author of every good mushroom book essentially forces the reader to identify the edible as well as the poisonous mushrooms by the color of their spore prints, and frowns upon those who just like to look at the pictures.

A notoriously poisonous species is illustrated on pages 48 and 60. Never taste these, and do not put them in the same container with the other mushrooms.

This introduction to mushrooms, in simple language, gives a flying start to using keys. Frederick and I eat 45 species of wild mushrooms, and every time we try a new species we *both* key it out—not consulting each other—in at least two books (see bibliography for suggestions).

Mushroom poisoning

If mushroom poisoning is suspected, get the patient to vomit without delay. Drinking warm mustard water or warm salt water may induce vomiting. Mustard water is preferable, for salt water may cause the poison to dissolve faster and hence get into one's system. (We have not had occasion to try these recipes.)

Drying mushrooms

Mushrooms, like babies, should only be washed if they are dirty. (Otherwise rough on the flavor or temperament respectively.) Pick your mushrooms clean, so there is no need to wash or trim them. Every time you reconstitute mushrooms, TASTE the water. Ninety percent of the flavor may be about to be thrown away if you don't taste. Most dried mushrooms taste better sautéed than boiled.

When the days have been damp, I have sometimes oven-dried mushrooms, but even with the lowest heat, the flavor never seemed to be as good as that of the air-dried mushrooms.

The following kinds can be air-dried by simply spreading them out so they do not touch each other: fairy rings, sulphur polypores, and oyster mushrooms.

These are best sliced before spreading out: puffball, boletus, chanterelle, morel, and honey cap.

Outdoor drying, especially in sunlight, is sometimes very quick and good, but one runs such a chance of having one's crop infested by maggots and beetles that indoor drying near a sunny screened window is often preferable. It is discouraging to gather a whole winter's supply of a favorite species and find that the insects have taken over on the drying trays. Large pieces of cardboard make good drying trays. Or you can string mushrooms like beads and hang them up near the ceiling.

If there are "worms" in some of the mushrooms on the drying tray, evidence of their presence can easily be detected on the smooth surface of the cardboard, and it is permissible to throw out the offending mushrooms. I assume one does not want to eat worms; and that they are not good for one. Both these assumptions, which are largely based on my upbringing, may be erroneous.

After the mushrooms are picked over and thoroughly dried, they may be stored in plastic bags, in ordinary paper bags, or even in canning jars.

PREPARING DRIED MUSHROOMS FOR COOKING

To prepare dried mushrooms for cooking, soak them in water or milk. Fairy rings take only 5 minutes, but some species take over an hour. The length of time needed to freshen mushrooms varies according to species and condition. Get them out of the water as soon as you can squeeze them like a sponge. Then cook them like fresh mushrooms.

For soup-making, I soak the mushrooms overnight, and may even boil the dried mushrooms. After all, for soups you want to get the flavor into the liquid.

Canning mushrooms (HELEN KABAT)

The Kabat family comes from Polish-American stock. The Poles take their mushrooms seriously and they have found their favorite species in the New World. One of these is the honey cap. When the honey caps are in season, parties of Polish-Americans pile out of the cities—Chicago, Detroit, Milwaukee, and Madison—and fill big baskets, often with only one species. At last I joined such a party and asked, "How can you use so many?" and the answer was, "They are for the whole year; we can them." Helen Kabat has supplied my favorite recipe.

CANNING HONEY CAPS

Mushrooms should be canned the day they are picked. The quicker they are canned after picking, the better the quality. Wash thoroughly, peel tough mushrooms, and immediately drop into cold water containing 1 tablespoon of vinegar per quart. Pre-cook by placing in a wire sieve or colander, cover with a lid, and immerse for 3 to 4 minutes in boiling water which contains 1 tablespoon vinegar and 1 teaspoon salt per quart.

Discoloration occurs if the hot mushrooms are exposed to air. Pack into cans or jars. Cover with freshly boiled water. Add 1 teaspoon of salt per quart. Seal cans hot. Process at 15 pounds pressure: No. 2 cans 20 minutes; No. 3 cans 25 minutes. For glass jars, process at 10 pounds pressure: quarts 35 minutes, pints 25 minutes.

Canned mushrooms take on the flavor of whatever they are cooked with, but taste bland unless they are cooked with other ingredients to give them flavor.

Drain well. Fry for about 20 minutes — long enough to dissipate the blandness — in plenty of drippings, bacon fat or shortening.

Canned mushrooms extend almost any kind of meat dish or meat substitute. I usually fry onions, then add the mushrooms, and then add them to whatever is used with the mushrooms, or just use them as a side dish. While frying onions, if I have celery, green peppers, etc., I add these to the onions and fry together, then add mushrooms.

Freezing mushrooms

Choose mushrooms free from spots and decay. Sort according to size. Trim off ends of stems. If mushrooms are larger than 1 inch across, slice them or cut them into quarters.

Mushrooms may be steamed or heated in fat in a frying pan.

To steam. Mushrooms to be steamed have better color if given anti-darkening treatment first.

Dip for 5 minutes in a solution containing 1 teaspoon lemon juice or 1½ teaspoons (4.5 grams) citric acid to a pint of water. Then steam.

Whole mushrooms (not larger than 1 inch across)	5 minutes
Buttons or quarters	3½ minutes
Slices	3 minutes

Cool promptly in cold water and drain.

To heat in pan. Heat small quantities of mushrooms in table fat in an open pan until almost done.

Cool in air or set pan in which mushrooms were cooked in cold water.

Pack into containers, leaving ½-inch head space. Seal and freeze.

Mushroom recipes

Cook about 20 minutes — longer if they are tough. Use only a little water, slightly salted, and save the water for soups, sauces, scrambled eggs, etc.

When frying or sautéing mushrooms, cook slowly over low heat, being careful not to let the fat get smoking hot.

In my opinion, mushrooms should be fried in butter, unless one is cooking one of the rather tasteless species.

Chanterelles, for example, are delicious fried in bacon fat in which partridges have been cooked. Pour the clear fat off and set it aside for other uses. Cook the mushrooms in a small amount of fat remaining in the bottom of the pan, which contains a delicious sediment—essence of partridge.

Mushrooms vary: some taste best merely fried until soft, others are better golden brown, and some benefit by being fried until crisp.

BROILED MUSHROOMS
(Smith 1938)

If wet, dry the caps with a paper towel. Place whole caps, gills up, on the broiler rack, dot with butter and sprinkle lightly with salt, place under the broiler in a preheated compartment, and broil until a golden brown or until somewhat crisp. If the caps are quite large it will be necessary to turn them and broil the other side also. This method of cooking is also adaptable to use over a camp fire. The mushrooms should be placed on the end of a peeled green stick or a long-handled fork and broiled over glowing coals.

MUSHROOM SAUCE
(Smith 1938)

Melt 6 tablespoons butter, add 4 tablespoons flour, blend till smooth; gradually add 2 cups chicken or meat broth and cook until creamy. Add 2 egg yolks or one whole egg beaten with ¼ cup rich milk or cream and one cup cooked mushrooms. Season with salt and pepper, add lemon juice, paprika or chopped parsley as desired.

Mushroom pie

Pie making is an art. It takes more than art lessons to make an artist and it takes more than recipes to make a pie-maker. The going rate for my pies is fifty-five dollars apiece, and furthermore, I am eager to share my secrets. (The first is a confession: an eccentric bachelor, who is in charge of a chemical lab, dotes on my pies and pays me back in chemical analyses in connection with my hawk research.)

The crust is of the essence and the same skill is needed for fruit pies, mushroom pies, or any pies.

PIE CRUST

¾ cup lard—or other shortening
About 2 cups flour
½ teaspoon salt

Lard varies; flour varies; temperature varies. It's just beyond me to circumvent these variations by dependence on recipes and measuring cups! Try to learn from a good pie-maker, rather than from a book. If this fails, learn to follow recipes as suggestions; vary them and do err on the side of more shortening and less water.

Temperature is most easily controlled: my shortening must be at room temperature. Lard fresh out of the refrigerator won't work into the flour properly, and runny lard seeps into the flour and produces a monotonous crust. Using a large dull knife or if you prefer, a pastry cutter, cut the lard into lightly salted flour. Work quickly until there is no loose flour, but stop before the dough becomes even-textured. Feel the dough between your fingers: heavy with lard, but not too greasy. Then add barely enough water to hold the dough together.

Lightly pat a wad of dough about the size of a small grapefruit into a ball and put it on a lightly floured wooden table. Modern, highly polished surfaces are too slippery for rolling out a good crust. If you don't have a wooden table, buy a square yard of naugahyde and roll out your crusts on it. Roll from the center toward the edges.

If your crust persists in cracking apart at the edges, start humming a little tune: your pie will not be pretty; it will probably be patched, and it is sure to be praised.

If, on the other hand, the edges remain smooth and pull back toward the center as you roll the crust out, there is little cause for rejoicing: you have been stingy with the lard and too liberal with the water, and it is too late to mend matters. Prick the top crust with a fork—to manufacture daisies, oak leaves, rabbits, or whatever design suits your fancy. Such crusts are manageable and easily decorated. They taste quite like cardboard and even polite guests tend to leave rather a lot of crust on their plates.

Shortening varies more than some people might suppose. Some commercial lards seem to be "padded" with water. If you have friends who butcher pigs, they may be happy to present you with big slabs of pig fat. (Fat from near the kidneys is best.) It is not much trouble to grind it up into small (bean-sized) pieces and render it by putting it on trays or pizza pans in your oven. Keep the temperature as low as possible and pour off your home-rendered lard from time to time. The little brownish fragments that are left over are "cracklings" and pleasant to nibble on.

You may be even more fortunate and have friends who have access to bear fat. Quite a number of bear hunters have heard about cholesterol, and just don't know what to do with bear lard. It makes the very best pie crusts of all.

MUSHROOM PIE FILLING
(Kate Dykema)

Filling for two 2-crust pies:
About 2 pounds mushrooms
1 pint heavy whipping cream*
4 beef bouillon cubes
4 tablespoons lemon juice
½ pint sour cream

*Whipping cream is now "ultra-pasteurized," which successfully removes all flavor. Good markets also carry "heavy (gourmet)" cream which is the same thing with the flavor left in.

Sauté mushrooms in butter, margarine, or any fat with a low melting point, such as goose or duck fat. Add whipping cream, beef bouillon cubes, lemon juice, and enough flour to thicken. (If you want it precise, ¼ cup, but flours vary.) Add sour cream—at least ½ pint—to taste.

For strong mushrooms like honey caps (*Armellaria melea*) or oyster mushrooms (*Pleurotus ostreatus*), add 1 pint sour cream. For less strong flavored mushrooms like fairy rings (*Marasmius oreades*), and those that are ordinarily obtainable at the supermarket, go easy on the sour cream.

There is no law against tasting your pie mixture before baking. The proportion of sour cream will bring your pie into balance.

This recipe is for *two* 12-inch pies. (One gets eaten too fast.)

Lard for pie crust used to come from the fat of a pig. It still should. Use real lard, or bear fat.

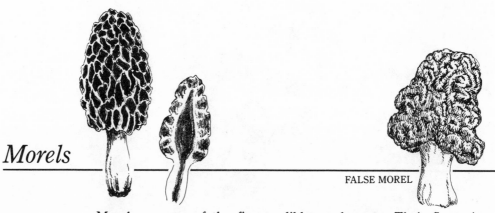

Morels

FALSE MOREL

Morels are one of the finest edible mushrooms. Their flavor is so outstanding that repeated attempts – all unsuccessful – have been made to grow them commercially. They have rather conical heads, a pleasant odor, and a hollow stem. Although there are several species, they are all edible so one need not feel it one's duty to tell them apart. *Note* that false morels bear a faint resemblance to morels. Their heads, however, are irregular and contorted and lack the distinctive *pitted* appearance of morels.

Until recently, an experienced mushroom hunter would no more tell where he gathered morels than he'd hang a note outside his back door telling burglars where he'd hidden the key. This has all changed in recent decades, not because people have become nicer, but because a small beetle carried a disease, introduced from Europe, from elm to elm in North America. The Dutch Elm Disease has been a boon to morels.

To find morels, look under dead elms and pass up those that no longer have bark clinging to parts of their branches. Don't just look near the trunk. Look where the elm cast the shadow of its former glory at noon, for this will lead you out to the dead root system on which these delectable fungi are thriving. Seek them when the wild asparagus is at its peak and the soil is moist. If you make a big haul share your booty, for dried or frozen morels have lost more than half of their flavor – the best half!

FRIED MORELS

Butter
Hot toast

Sauté slowly in real butter until golden brown, and serve on toast.

Oyster mushroom

These whitish or tending to fawn color or grey shelf mushrooms ordinarily grow in clusters on decaying poplars or willows and sometimes on other hardwoods. The shelves are roughly kidney shaped and are sometimes attached to the tree or stump by a poor excuse for a stem on one side. The elm mushroom (*Pleurotus ulmarius*) does have a substantial stem, but it is so like the oyster mushroom (*P. ostreatus*) that they are now considered to be one species. The spore print is dull lilac, although may appear white if only a thin dusting is obtained. The gills are white.

These mushrooms are often to be found in great abundance at about the time that the wild grape is in bloom, and sometimes again in the autumn. Armed with a long stick to knock them down from the dead poplars, one can sometimes gather two bushels in an hour. Oyster mushrooms are usually delicious, but occasionally one encounters a clump which, although edible, is no particular treat. The factors which influence the taste of individual oyster mushroom clumps are still something of an enigma. The best oyster mushrooms I ever gathered came from a large open-grown cottonwood which had been dead so long that only a few fragments of bark remained on its silvery trunk. I encountered a distinctly mediocre clump on a not long dead large-toothed aspen in shady oak woods, but I've found very good ones on similar trees.

This good eating mushroom is the only mushroom I've ever had occasion to shoot. It sometimes grows so high on such rotten old trees that shooting is the only solution. It grows, usually singly, on old elms and box-elders, emerging from dead wood and from tree holes. As a rule one can knock each individual down with a stick. I have even found them growing on roots, so I crawled around on my hands and knees to get a basketful.

Although one is most apt to find oyster mushrooms in the autumn, I have gathered them when cruising on snowshoes in early winter. They are good fried or used in general cooking. They may be either dried or canned. To dry oyster mushrooms, one can string them on a stout string with an upholsterer's needle and hang the strings up indoors to dry.

Fairy rings

Fairy rings have a special quality, which no other mushroom in this book has to quite the same degree. Not only are they the most easily dried, but also they have an astonishing, and gratifying, proclivity for regaining their moisture. Dried fairy rings, placed in water and squeezed a few times, are ready to cook like fresh mushrooms within five minutes.

Shrivelling up and expanding again is natural to fairy rings, and although it is easier to gather them after a rain when they are conspicuous and plump, it is perfectly possible to gather them during a severe drought, after one has learned to identify them when dry. Fairy rings grow in open fields. Rather similar looking mushrooms growing in the shade are a different species and not recommended for eating. Neither should one eat those "fairy rings" which smell like garlic, nor those with wooly stems.

Fairy rings are to be found throughout the spring, summer, and autumn, but the best time to gather a winter supply is when the bluegrass seed is ripe and the wild strawberries are fruiting. This is often a time of peak production of fresh new caps, easy to find in grassy places. Once the first mushroom is found one follows the ring until one has completed the entire circle, gathering and pushing aside the grass to find more as one crawls.

Small rings are young and large ones are old, for rings start in the center and grow outwards, and one can find these rings year after year . . . always a little larger. I know of fairy rings more than fifteen feet in diameter, but cannot hazard a guess as to their age, as I don't know their average annual growth rate for this region.

It is easier to take along a pair of scissors and cut off the mushrooms when gathering dry ones, as the stems are tough and hard to break. If one just pulls them up, one not only has to go to the trouble of cutting the stems anyway, but also of scrubbing away the earth from the entire collection before cooking.

Suitable for omelettes, soups, stews, or sautéed.

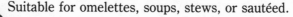

Puffballs

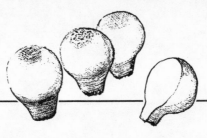

Puffballs are to be found in a great variety of habitats; on rotten logs, in piles of leaves, in deep woods, in driveways, and in meadows so sparse and sterile that the appearance of anything so monstrous and delicious seems uncanny. It is in the deep lush woods that the small ones grow, and in the unlikely looking bare places in abused meadows that I have found the great Giant Puffballs—sometimes as big as cauliflower heads.

Although there are quite a few species of puffballs, this group is an exception to the rule that one must know the species before eating. The beginner might mistake young, not fully formed mushrooms of other species for puffballs, but these, upon being cut open will not be homogeneous in texture and the stem within will be apparent.

Never eat a "puffball" if it is not even textured throughout and white— like the inside of a marshmallow—all the way through. Some are purple inside; avoid them. (The white ones turn cream colored, and then later dark brown and powdery with age.)

Puffballs should be eaten fairly promptly—not kept for days, as this darkening process, which is a step toward spore formation, can set in soon after they are gathered. Keep them in a cool place to retard darkening.

PUFFBALL SALAD

Dice the puffballs and add them to a tossed salad; or eat them raw.

FRIED PUFFBALLS

Slice in ½ inch slices, dip in egg, flour lightly, salt, and fry until soft like eggplant. Tiny puffballs need only be cut in half.

DRIED PUFFBALLS

Puffballs continue to ripen after they are picked. They may become inedible. Part of one's booty is apt to be lost if one leaves them lying around hoping to attend to them "presently." Slice them promptly and slice them thin (¼ inch or less). I have found air drying at ordinary room temperature satisfactory.

Dried puffballs may be soaked ½ hour in water and cooked like fresh ones, or they may be salted and eaten raw.

FROZEN PUFFBALLS

Puffballs can be kept a week or two in the freezing compartment of a refrigerator and upon being thawed out they are as good as ever. No wrapping or precooking is necessary for short time storage. The most convenient way to save them over a long period is drying.

Boletus

These mushrooms have the common cap and central stem shape, but instead of having gills beneath the cap, there are many tiny tubes. The famous and much sought after European *Steinpilz* belongs to this genus. *It is not safe* to gather Boletus simply because one is familiar with the European species. According to George Knudsen, State Naturalist of Wisconsin for 25 years, "None of the 85 or so boletes are deadly, but a couple (red tube mouths and instant blue) are somewhat poisonous. Others may be bitter." I will give a description of one good species and suggest that those who wish to learn more, study one of the comprehensive mushroom books listed in the bibliography.

Edible Boletus. This species is ordinarily found in woods, and sometimes becomes very abundant in young pine plantations. The tubes are separable from the cap. The spores are yellowish to brown or black. The stem is smooth, not shaggy or furrowed. The tubes are yellow or brown, but *not* red or reddish. The cut or scarred surface does *not* turn blue.

There are two distinct schools of thought on the subject of cooking Boletus. One method is to simply fry the entire mushroom. The tubular portion turns to a delicate oyster-like texture which some people find particularly delicious. Others consider this oyster-like quality of the tubes a slimy mess, and remove all the tubular portion from each mushroom before cooking.

Boletus may be dried for winter use, but they must be sliced thin and should be dried in sunlight and in good drying weather. They are excellent canned.

Shaggymanes

The shaggymane is so distinctive in appearance, that after studying the illustration, one should have no difficulty in identifying it. These mushrooms never become parasol shaped, but remain conical. The shaggy appearance of the surface is characteristic. The ring may be on the stem or may have disappeared. The spores are black, and the whole mushroom melts down to an inky mass if not gathered when it is young.

Shaggymanes are apt to occur on lawns, in fields, and in such places as dumps behind greenhouses.

These are delicate and perishable mushrooms. Delay as little as possible before cooking them. They may start to turn black in an hour or so. Select fresh young heads, and if they have started to darken, trim away the blackish parts.

Sauté in butter being careful not to overcook. These should never be fried until hard . . . a golden brown is ideal.

Not suitable for drying.

Amanita (poisonous)

Beware this group, but learn to recognize these mushrooms, for they closely resemble some of the edible species, and it is well to be able to recognize some of the commonest of the most poisonous species. The very names of the amanitas are suggestive—"destroying angel," "death cup." Amanitas have the following characteristics:

1) Spore print white;
2) Gills do not touch the stem;
3) Ring (this can crumble and disappear in old individuals);
4) Volva (sometimes this is a well-formed cup, but sometimes it is reduced to mere fragmentary particles). When gathering an unfamiliar species, one should dig the mushroom up carefully, and look for the volva at the base of the stem. One should view the mushroom with suspicion even if there is but a suggestion of a volva, and not even taste it.

See page 48 for parts of a mushroom on which points 2, 3, and 4 are illustrated.

Honey caps

In several regions these are called shoestring mushrooms; they are the most highly prized of the autumn mushrooms, and are noted for their fine flavor. Alexander Smith (1938), however, writes, "It is collected extensively in the Detroit area. Apparently the disagreeable flavor disappears if the caps are parboiled!" I have *never* encountered a honey cap with a poor flavor, nor have I tasted those from the Detroit area, which sound discouraging.

Years ago I gathered my honey caps from rotting stumps of oaks and other hardwoods. They always grew in clumps. Then that mixed blessing, the Dutch Elm Disease, killed our elms. All over the lawn under where the elms had once lifted their arched branches, mushrooms that looked rather like honey caps appeared. John Kubsiak, a biologist and a honey cap enthusiast, came to my rescue over the telephone. "Honey caps!" Then he added, "Did you say you have more than you can use? Bushels? We'll be right over."

They do not have cups at the base of the stems like those on the deadly amanitas, but they often have a filmy, but fairly distinct ring not far beneath the cap. The caps, which often have a rather slimy surface, especially when young, vary from honey colored to dark brown or almost black.

The gills sometimes taper downward on the stem, the spores are white, and the meat, also white, has a slightly bitter taste if nibbled raw.

As a rule frying is recommended. Stewed honey caps are very mild; they take on the flavor of whatever they are cooked with.

Canned honey caps are outstanding. Although they may be successfully dried if sliced thin, it seems a pity not to can any one can spare for winter use. (See page 51.)

Sulphur polypore

These first-rate shelf mushrooms are easily identified. They grow on wood, either on standing trees, stumps or fallen logs, and most commonly on oaks. The gaudy clusters of orange-yellow flaring shelves are conspicuous and hardly to be mistaken for anything else. The under surface is covered with minute pores which look like velvet. The meat is white.

They are good fried. One clump often supplies enough for several meals (single shelves may be about a foot wide). One can use the thinner portions of each shelf for an epicurean dish, fried in butter. The thicker parts of each shelf are also good but require longer cooking, and are a fine addition to stews and gravy.

Each autumn the same polypore stumps fruit anew. Go back year after year to gather more.

They are easily dried, and although they dry rather slowly, one does not even need to cut or break them to dry them at room temperature indoors.

POLYPORE SOUP

About 4 cups of sulphur polypore (other mushrooms are worth trying)
Salted water
1 tablespoon flour
2 tablespoons butter or fat
1 10-ounce can of gravy or 1 cup beef gravy
½ cup cream or evaporated milk
Pinch of garlic powder

Fresh polypores can be made into soup directly. Dried polypores are best soaked in water 6 to 12 hours. Boil the polypore meat in slightly salted water until the texture of tender chicken breast meat is achieved. This takes about ¾ of an hour for moderately tough polypores.

Stir a tablespoon of flour into about two tablespoons of hot fat until blended. Then slowly add the water the mushrooms were cooked in. Run the meat through a fine meat grinder. Combine all the ingredients and heat before serving, but do not bring to a boil again.

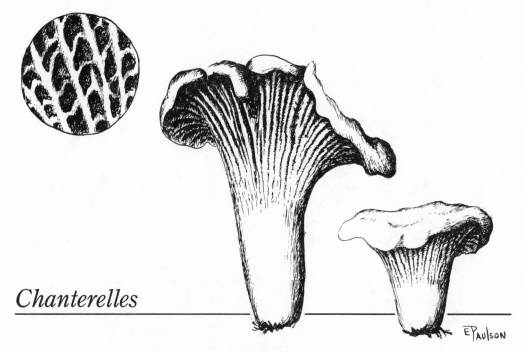

E Paulson

Chanterelles

The gills of chanterelles look almost like folds and bear only a superficial resemblance to the almost paper-like gills of most kinds of gill mushrooms.

The funnel-shaped cap, with its turned down edge, the fold-like, usually forking gills, and the bright egg yolk yellow of the entire mushroom (cap, gills, and stem) make this mushroom easy to identify.

These mushrooms are essentially identical in flavor to the European chanterelle and grow in similar sites on both continents, namely under conifers or hardwoods.

Often one catches sight of only one or two of the bright yellow caps, practically smothered by last year's fallen leaves, but a persistent hunt, pushing away leaves in the vicinity, may yield a nice basket of chanterelles, for they are often gregarious. Note: they do not grow in clumps like the yellow and *poisonous* Jack-o'-lantern mushrooms. These are illustrated side by side on page 73.

Chanterelles lose flavor if cooked too quickly. Sauté slowly and serve as an accompaniment to meat. The perfect combination is chanterelles and woodcock, for the flavor of each complements the other admirably.

Creamed chanterelles on toast make a fine supper dish.

At the time that the blueberry crop is at its height in mid-summer, chanterelles begin to appear and they may be found well into the autumn; even as late as the beginning of the leaf fall of the aspens, so they are among the species which can be served fresh with game.

To dry chanterelles, cut the larger ones in two, and spread them out on a tray with the smaller ones, which will dry perfectly well if left intact.

AUTUMN

Autumn, when grass turns brown and popples are
tinged with gold, is the time of abundance. It is the
hunting season and the ways of hunters are
various. Thousands look forward to the whirring
wingbeat of a flushed partridge, the silhouettes of
ducks stringing across the sky, the fragrance of
damp leaves and the chill of night lifted by sunrise.
Some will learn from the wind and the weather and
the game they hunt; their perceptions will become
heightened and with respect comes understanding.
Others remain shooters only. Those who shoot only
to brag about getting the limit are as lost as those
with the money madness upon them.

State and federal laws regulate the kill so that a species will not be endangered over a large area. Upon the individual sportsman rests the responsibility of not taking too many, though he may be within his legal rights if he shoots until the last of a flock is dead.

There are some whose tender-heartedness is so great that they would not kill a fly, yet they drain a marsh, burn a thicket, or plant up an opening without weighing the consequences. Whole generations of ducks, the call of rails and the thunder-pumping of bitterns are abolished with the lost marsh; a quail covey may die out the winter after the thicket is burned. Perhaps in spring one once more hears the whistle "Bob White," but it is only a mimic starling echoing the call of a covey that is no more. If it was a sharptail opening that was planted to trees, the birds will not disappear immediately. In spring the cocks will still assemble to dance and coo and fight in the early mornings, and in the summer the hens will wander among small trees with their broods of striped young, but in five to eight years they will be gone.

To some the loss of range is neither a clear nor dramatic concept. Loss of range is homelessness. It can extirpate a species more effectively than a plague. A plague tends to leave at least a few resistant individuals . . . loss of range can obliterate a population outright.

It is no coincidence that great hunters have often been great conservationists, for it is things like these that hunters learn. They know too the rich abundance of autumn when game populations are at their annual peak.

The beginning of the hunt is the time for speculation. Will the woodcocks come into our alder swale which has lain unpastured for two years, or has the new rank growth destroyed their feeding grounds? Will the early flight of ducks be fishy? And the deer—with the bumper crop of acorns to feast on—won't even the neck of an ancient buck be a company treat?

Mayapple or mandrake

Mayapples are common in rich woods and pastures. Their yellowish, rubbery, jointed rootstocks are poisonous. The leaves—not quite as poisonous as the roots—should not be eaten.

After mayapples are in bloom, the petals fall and the pistil expands greenly all summer long. By early autumn the ripe fruits are yellow, and as big as a small lemon. Their slightly acid sweet pulp is good raw or as marmalade.

Wild grapes

Wild grape vines grow along hedgerows and often in rich woods. Aldo Leopold once suggested that quail covies could find excellent shelter if farmers simply cut down trees that supported grape vines. This is a practical innovation, not only giving quail security, but also making it easier for us to gather quantities of grapes within easy reach.

JELLY

Wild grapes make excellent jelly. Pick them when between 1/8 to 1/4 of the grapes are still hard, greenish and under ripe. These contain enough pectin so that it is possible to make pure wild grape jelly. Boil until the seeds and skins separate easily (about a half an hour), strain, and—using equal parts of sugar and juice—cook for 5 minutes.

But if the grapes are already ripe it is advisable to use commercial pectin, or add a few green apples to make the jelly jell.

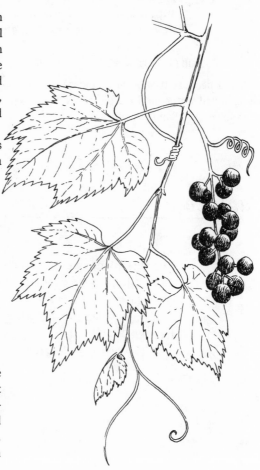

SPICED GRAPES
(Carolyn Errington)

6½ pounds grapes
3½ pounds sugar
1 pint cider vinegar
2 teaspoons cinnamon
2 teaspoons cloves
½ teaspoon salt

Separate pulp of grapes from skins. Press the pulp through a strainer to eliminate seeds. (It is well to boil the pulp until it is soft to facilitate straining.) Make syrup of sugar and vinegar. Boil 15 minutes. Skim. Add skins, pulp and spices to syrup. Boil ½ hour from the time a full rolling boil is reached.

Jerusalem artichoke

The potato-like tubers of this sunflower have a fine artichoke flavor. The plant was cultivated by the North American Indians. As early as the seventeenth century, it was introduced to Europe for cultivation. It derives its name from the Italian "girasole" – turning to the sun – which later became "Jerusalem."

Rich moist thickets often harbor great patches of these hardy perennials. Dig the tubers after the tops have become dry in the autumn. Unlike potatoes, they are not easily stored. The Indians ate them raw, but we prefer them cooked.

BOILED ARTICHOKE

Wash and peel the tubers. Slice and cook in boiling salted water until tender. Serve with lemon juice or hollandaise sauce.

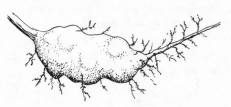

Bugleweed

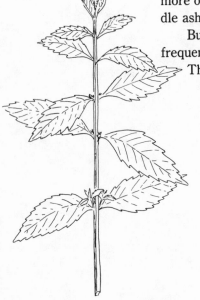

For this plant, we sometimes have to compete with muskrats. But more often, as we canoe past rat houses, we spot bugleweed and paddle ashore to gather some.

Bugleweed grows in the sort of moist open places that muskrats frequent.

The crisp, underground tubers are good raw.

Highbush cranberry

Highbush cranberry is not a cranberry at all. It is a tall shrub most often found in low places, frequently among alders or willows. The scarlet berries, ripening in autumn, hang in clusters. In a good year individual bushes may be fairly ablaze with the berries and just one bush may yield several pints of jelly. Each berry has a large, flat seed.

JELLY

Cook up the berries with just enough water so they do not scorch. When they are soft enough to be pulpy, strain through a piece of cloth. Cook these juices down with about equal parts of sugar to facilitate jelling.

JAM

After the first heavy frosts the berries tend to shrivel a little, but their flavor is not impaired and now, at last, one can pop the seeds out without much trouble, and make jam. Boil seeded berries adding sugar to taste. Highbush cranberry jam requires rather less sugar than most fruits as the berries are particularly sweet after the frost has been upon them.

Nannyberry

Nannyberries have the flattened seeds which characterize the Viburnums. The berries are blue-black and sweet with a raisin taste. They may be used as above, or dried for winter use. They are easily dried at room temperature. It is not practical to remove the seeds before drying. When the time comes to use them, boil the berries until the pulp is easily separated from the seeds, add sugar to taste, and make sauce or jam.

Acorns

According to Yanovsky (1936), the North American Indians used acorns extensively for food. "To remove the astringent and bitter principles, the acorns were dried and ground and the meal was percolated with water until it tasted sweet. The sweet meal was prepared for food in many ways."

The white oak group (including bur oak) does not have bristles on the teeth of the leaves and the acorns are good eaten raw like nuts.

The red and black oaks have bristles on the teeth of the leaves and their acorns are bitter and require a good deal of preparation. One of the easiest ways of telling these two major groups of oaks apart is to taste the acorns. If they taste good, eat them.

BUR OAK

WHITE OAK PATTIES

Acorns
Egg
Fat
Salt

Boil dried acorns until soft. Drain and grind. (I use a meat grinder.) Salt lightly and mix with enough egg to form patties. Fry like pancakes.

JACK OAK PATTIES

Jack oak patties never taste quite as good, and another step is needed. After grinding and draining the acorns, they need to be percolated about 20 minutes to remove bitterness. I use a coffee percolator. Children enjoy making jack oak patties.

WHITE OAK

RED OAK

GAME BIRDS

How to tell the age of game birds

One can examine feet, poke breastbones, and lift by the bill to see whether or not it breaks and come up with some sort of a guess. Depending upon one's skill and opportunities to exercise it, one's guess may be very good or very bad. I once watched an old sharptail hunter separate a pile of birds into old and young. He barely glanced at them, ignored the wing moult, and had never heard of the bursa, and he was right in every case. He said, "I just do it by the look of them. My wife wants to know how long to cook them."

This is precisely what most of us want to know. There is now one really satisfactory method of separating young "birds of the year" from old birds. The Bursa of Fabricius, a noticeable, but small sac inside the vent under the tail is found only in young birds. It was first discovered by Fabricius in 1621, but this important discovery was essentially lost, buried in the literature, for 300 years.

In 1939 Carl Gower wrote of the bursa, "Game investigators, ornithologists, taxidermists, and laboratory workers are often called upon to estimate or judge the age of birds when preparing them as specimens or performing autopsies or other examinations."

He failed to mention cooks!

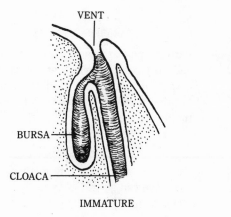

IMMATURE

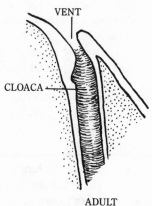

ADULT

General instructions for preparing

To prepare a bird for the oven pluck, cut off head, wing tips, and feet, fold back the neck skin to remove the crop, then draw. The abdominal incision should be just large enough so that one can pull out the gizzard and intestines. The kidneys lie in shallow hollows on either side of the back bone and these too, should be removed. Peeling the gizzard is rather like getting the stone out of a peach; cut down through the first layer only of the hard part. As in the case of a peach, save the outside. The gall bladder is a small, ordinarily green sac, projecting from a lobe of the liver. Remove it, being careful not to break it as the acrid flavor of its juice will persist on any meat that it touches. You will not always be able to find a gall bladder.

If the intestines have been broken inside the bird, wash out the body cavity with cold water. Never wash or soak meat unless there is a good reason for doing so. The whole point of cleaning a bird is to remove unpleasant flavors—not to destroy the taste of the meat!

Gut-shot birds do not keep as well—eat them first.

Methods of plucking

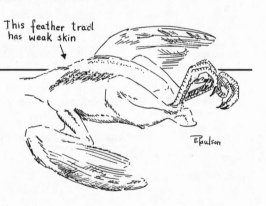

This feather tract has weak skin

DRY PLUCKING

Epicures often insist on this method. Pull the feathers off with a quick jerking motion, being careful not to tear the skin.

On upland game birds, the skin unfortunately often is torn along the large feather tracts over the breast where the feathers are relatively large and the skin is rather weak.

Along these tracts, hold the bases of the feathers, plucking only a few at a time.

Duck, coot, and goose feathers and down are high quality sleeping bag and pillow stuffing. After the feathers have been removed, roll the down off with your thumb.

SCALDING

To loosen the feathers, plunge the bird into hot, not boiling, water for a minute or so. Pluck as soon as cool enough to handle.

PARAFFIN TREATMENT

Partially pluck the bird. Heat a pan of water and melt paraffin, which will float, in it. To coat the bird with paraffin, dip it in the liquid. Let the paraffin cool, and then scrape it and the feathers off.

SINGEING

No matter which plucking method has been used, one can get rid of extra "hairs" or fluff by singeing.

Ruffed grouse or partridge

Partridges, unlike prairie grouse, never improve with ripening. They are best eaten soon after they are killed lest the legs and back become strong. The kidneys have an exceptionally strong flavor and should be removed with thoroughness.

ROAST PARTRIDGE

Pluck, dress and clean. Place on a small open dish (a pie plate is ideal for two partridges) thus saving every drop of juice to pour over the birds when serving. Bake 20 minutes in a hot oven (475°).

Partridges, like other light-breasted game birds, are extraordinarily difficult to prepare for the table, for they should be cooked through, but if they are the least bit overdone, the meat becomes tasteless, stringy and dry.

How to stuff a partridge.

Modern taxidermists have developed skills unknown in the olden days. So have modern cooks. This is about cooking: what to put inside a partridge to make it taste good. Partridge stuffing should be moist. An apple or an onion will do, but chanterelle stuffing is more delectable.

CHANTERELLE STUFFING

Fry chanterelles slowly in lightly salted shortening until they are limp, rather than crisp. Stuff each bird with this mixture. (I have so often flushed partridges where the chanterelles grow that I've suspected partridges of stuffing *themselves* with these mushrooms!)

The chanterelle is the famous "Pfifferling" served in Europe's finest restaurants. The Jack-o'-lantern, similarly colored, is a spooky mushroom. I wouldn't eat it. It glows in the dark, but its reputation is such that—although it is not apt to kill you—I'd never stuff a partridge with it.

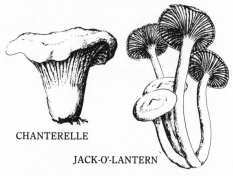

CHANTERELLE

JACK-O'-LANTERN

I might take a young one home, turn out the lights and hope it would glow for the children and me.

FRIED PARTRIDGE

Cut the partridge in half lengthwise, dip in flour, and fry, being careful not to overcook it. If you want to peek to see whether or not it is done, cut into the thickest part of the breast muscle. If it is not quite done, increase the cut and the partridge will finish cooking in a matter of moments after the hot fat gets a chance to penetrate the interior of the breast. Salt before serving. Older birds are sometimes better braised.

BRAISED PARTRIDGE

Partridge, cut up
Flour
Salt pork or bacon fat
4–5 carrots, scrubbed and sliced
1 onion, peeled and chopped
Thyme
1 bay leaf
Salt, pepper, and paprika to taste
Water with bouillon cube
   or chicken stock

Cut bird into pieces and dust with flour. In a deep pan sauté in salt pork or bacon fat with carrots and onion. When nicely browned, add spices and cover with water or stock. Bake until meat is tender (40 minutes to 1½ hours at 350°). As soon as the meat is done, take it out and put it where it will stay warm. It is also time to start heating up the platter.

Taste the gravy makings. If the flavor is right, add water only. If the gravy tastes flat, add meat stock, spiced salt, or bouillon cubes. Pour gravy over the meat at the last moment and be sure to serve it hot.

Sharp-tailed grouse

Sharptails are outstanding table birds. Unlike most gallinaceous birds such as pheasant and ruffed grouse, they retain their juices well and do not tend to dry out while cooking.

Very young birds, still in the juvenal plumage, have light breast meat of delicate texture but the flavor is still undeveloped. By October, almost all the birds are in prime condition, with breast meat dark, almost like the legs, and very delicious.

Sharptails should be served rare or at most medium well-done.

ROAST SHARPTAIL

Pluck dry, dress and clean. Do not stuff. Roast in a hot oven (450°) 25 minutes for medium-rare sharptails.

FRIED SHARPTAIL

Pluck, dress, and clean. Cut in pieces for frying. The breasts of these birds are so plump that it is often simpler to cut them away from the bone; then cut or divide each side of the breast into two pieces. If this is not done, the legs and back will be overdone while the breast still requires more cooking. Flour each piece lightly before placing it in the hot fat. Salt just before serving.

If you want to take the wild taste out of your grouse, pay no attention to anything I've written.

Wild turkey

Wild turkeys became scarce over much of the United States a few decades ago, and the art of turkey hunting almost died out. Game managers successfully reintroduced these large wary creatures in many states—a heartening success story.

The art of turkey cooking didn't die out because domestic turkeys, aided by supermarkets, certainly kept the tradition of turkey eating alive. For *roast turkey* and *left-over turkey* I will just refer you to your favorite cookbooks. For some mysterious reason, fried turkey is seldom given credit for being a most delicious dish.

FRIED TURKEY

Cut the bird into pieces about the size of a domestic chicken's thigh. Set aside the bones, the giblets, the neck, and the *drumsticks* for soup. Each drumstick has annoying little splints—they are really ossified tendons—and it is much easier to pull them out of a soup stock in the kitchen than to pick away at them with a knife and fork at the dinner table.

Flour
Turkey (cut up)
Fat
Salt and pepper

Dust the meat lightly with flour. Fry 35 minutes in hot fat covered, then 5 to 10 minutes more to brown.

BRAISED TURKEY

Same ingredients as above. Same recipe too, except if you are about to eat a tough, old tom, add a cup of water to the fried turkey and cook until tender.

Pheasant

Pheasants may be roasted, fried, or braised (see partridge for suitable ingredients). Recipes for domestic chicken are also acceptable for pheasant.

ROAST PHEASANT

Pheasants, unlike partridges, are best roasted in a slow oven (350°) twenty minutes per pound. A good stuffing, especially with celery, adds to the flavor. Pheasants should be plucked for roasting. They may either be plucked dry, or first scalded by plunging for a moment or two into almost boiling water before taking off the feathers.

FRIED PHEASANT

Young pheasants are excellent fried (see recipe for partridge). They may either be plucked or skinned.

BRAISED PHEASANT

(See braised partridge.) Old birds may require up to two hours at 350°. They may be plucked or skinned.

POACHED PHEASANT
(Philleo Nash)

1 pheasant (cut into about 10 pieces)
3 chicken bouillon cubes
1 heaping tablespoon creamy salad dressing
Black pepper
Red pepper (cayenne)
Margarine
Flour

Pheasants have such big breasts that it pays to cut each breast in half. Otherwise the legs and back will be overdone and dry before the breast meat is cooked through and has lost its pinkness. Marinate the cut up pheasant in 1½ quarts water, seasoned with 3 bouillon cubes, salad dressing (whatever brand you like), black pepper, and red pepper for 1 to 3 hours. Bring to a boil and simmer for 15 minutes. Take out the meat and boil the marinade until there is about ½ quart left. In the meantime, cool the meat, remove the bones, and cut the meat into bite-sized pieces. Set them aside. In a large frying pan, melt 2 tablespoons margarine, add 2 tablespoons flour, stir for 3 or 4 minutes, and then gradually add the marinade. Taste this gravy. Season to taste. Add the meat, and serve.

IMPROVED PHEASANT

Pheasants have one advantage over our native game birds. They have so little flavor (less than domestic chicken, by far) that, cooked simply, they serve as a nice, bland substrate for sauces.

1 pheasant (cut into about 10 pieces)
¼ cup butter

Bone the bird. Sauté 10 minutes in butter. Add ⅛ cup water, and simmer ½ hour.

In the meantime make a Bearnaise sauce. We use:

¼ cup red wine (burgundy)*
1 onion (chopped fine)
½ teaspoon each of oregano, coriander, and thyme

---

*Bearnaise sauce made with white wine is more traditional. Red wine makes a more robust sauce. As pheasant flesh has little flavor, it benefits from a less delicate sauce.

(Boil these over medium heat until reduced to two teaspoons. Strain, and set aside.)

4 egg yolks
1 cup butter (2 sticks)

Beat egg yolks in a pot until thick. Heat slowly over hot water or over very low heat, keep adding tablespoon-sized pieces of butter and keep beating the mixture with a wire whisk. If you get impatient and want to speed up the process, increase the heat a trifle and beat furiously. If you have a favorite way of making hollandaise sauce, use it.

Once the hollandaise is completed, beat in the reduced wine-onion-spices mixture. Pour this over the simmered pheasant pieces and serve.

Dove

The dove is America's Number One game bird. Birdwatchers and ornithologists call it the Mourning Dove because of its sweet, sad cooing. The sweet, sad cooing is a territorial declaration—telling other doves to keep away. This "bird of love" actually does a lot of fighting. Most, if not all, of the fighting, however, is for love's sake.

The flesh of the dove is dark and tender. Some find doves small, but I feel . . .

> The dove is larger
> Than the oyster.
> It's tastier;
> The oyster's moister.

Doves are one of the easiest birds to pluck: the feathers almost seem to fall out. But in the South, it is customary to skin doves. Some only eat the breasts. I have never found their legs, backs, and necks strong—just bony, and fine for soup stock or gravy.

ROAST DOVE

Preheat oven to 450°. Pluck the doves, eviscerate them and roast them whole for 10 minutes at 450°. (They look like miniature turkeys.)

DOVE BREASTS

Dot a shallow pan with one tablespoon of margarine per dove. Put the breasts of each dove on its little mound of margarine. Roast them 9 minutes at 450° in a preheated oven.

Hungarian partridge* and quail

These may be cooked like partridge but the cooking times should be reduced as follows: Roast 15 minutes at 475°. If birds have been skinned, roast 12 minutes at 450°. Braise 35 minutes at 350°.

BROILED HUNGARIAN PARTRIDGE OR BROILED QUAIL

Split the birds down the back. Arrange birds skin side down on a preheated broiler about 4 inches from heat. Broil about 20 minutes. In the meantime, fry the giblets in butter, first putting in the gizzards; when these are almost done, add hearts, liver and mushrooms. Prepare hot toast, pour fried giblets and mushrooms over the toast, place the birds on top and garnish with water cress.

ZACHRY RANCH QUAIL
(Phil Evans)

In Texas, it is customary to skin quail, rather than plucking them. Zachry Ranch quail are split up the back, and have their entire backbone, including the tail, removed. This leaves the whole breast and both legs loosely attached to each other.

4 quail
Flour—for dusting
4 slices of bacon
Salt and pepper

Dust the quail lightly in flour. Fry 10 minutes in bacon fat. Then add about ½ inch of water, cover the pan, and *steam* the birds about 10 minutes. Add more water if needed for steaming. Put the quail on plates.

Stir about 2 tablespoons of flour into the pan. Season with salt and pepper. Add water stirring constantly until the gravy is nice and thick, but pours easily.

I suggest serving Zachry Ranch quail with wild rice and pouring the gravy over the rice.

---

*Hunters normally call these swift flying birds of the open country "Hungarian partridges" or "huns." Ornithologists prefer to call them "gray partridges."

Woodcock

It is well known that Leopold took time to go hunting, not only with his family, but with his students as well. It is less well known that he was an excellent cook. I wrote down some of his recipes and still remember the day that "roast woodcock" went into my file.

We were hunting partridges in Adams County, near the Roche-a-Cri: Aldo and his students, Hammy and I. The partridge hunting was rather poor, but we both recall three remarks he made that day. I pushed – again and again – through the brambles bare-legged, hoping to jump a bird from some sunny dust bath. Leopold said, "Fran is never happier than when her legs are all scratched up." He was pleased with his girl graduate student.

Then Hammy came to a fence – and stopped for moment or two, standing perfectly still. A partridge burst from a hazel. Hammy swung and dropped it neatly with his 20 gauge. Leopold said, "Isn't it funny? Some people are always caught just crossing a fence when a bird flushes."

Leopold's praise was seldom obvious. He had not said, "Fran is a good sport." Nor had he explained that it was nice to be hunting with someone who knew that gamebirds get uneasy when they can't hear you moving. It pays to be in shooting position whenever you stop, rather than with your gun on the ground and a leg on each side of a fence.

Aldo and the two Hamerstroms crossed the fence into a small rather dry woods, which we would all call the "woodcock woods" thereafter.

Leopold asked, "What makes those timberdoodles come in here?"

We shot our supper and enough for lunch. We never did discover why the timberdoodles selected that particular woodlot, but that evening Aldo taught me how to cook them.

Woodcock—and jacksnipe—are not cooked like other game, for it is correct to roast them with their insides in.

Just as part of the digestive tract of the lobster makes an excellent sauce to accompany the meat, so do woodcock and jacksnipe intestines add to a perfectly roasted little bird.

A number of otherwise estimable people who bite into sausages, cased in intestines, without a second thought, boggle at even tasting the intestines of these sweet little birds. For these, half way measures are suggested. Do not cut into the body cavity and let the meat dry out. Simply remove all the feathers and roast the birds whole. If some of your guests leave the intestines on the plate along with the bones, it is their loss. Epicures of the older generation served such small game with the heads on. For one thing many felt that it did not look right headless on the platter and besides, the brains are tasty.

ROAST WOODCOCK
(Aldo Leopold)

Salt lightly and roast 15 minutes in a hot oven (450°).

BROILED WOODCOCK

Split the birds, broil like quail, and serve on toast. Chanterelles are especially good with woodcock.

FRIED WOODCOCK

Split, dip in flour and fry.

JACKSNIPE

Cook the same way.

Wild rice

Although the great rice beds of the United States are largely gone, wild rice, upon which the Indians used to depend, is still harvested by them in some states. In other states, like California, it is now grown commercially and has driven down the price the Indians in the Lake States are getting for theirs.

This excellent grain is gathered from boats in the autumn, then dried or lightly parched to facilitate hulling, and cooked in a variety of ways.

Parching is said to bring out the best flavor, and also reduces the cooking time.

Wild rice can be hulled and cooked after it has been sun-dried for one day.

BOILED WILD RICE

To plenty of boiling, salted water add a handful per person. Cook until soft (20 minutes to an hour). One should use enough water so the kernels stay separate and are not permitted to become soggy.

POPPED OR PARCHED WILD RICE
(Clyde Terrell)

Deep fat or cooking oil
Fine wire strainer
Butter
Salt

Heat deep fat until it smokes slightly. Then put strainer in fat and sprinkle 1 to 3 tablespoons of uncooked wild rice into it. Wild rice pops and swells about three times in bulk. Let brown slightly after all has popped. Requires about 2 minutes. Repeat until you have desired amount. Drain and serve with salt and melted butter. Serve like nuts or with meat.

(Also may be prepared in a pan without strainer, using just enough hot fat or bacon drippings to cover wild rice.)

Pigeon

Not all pigeons are wild. Some of the pigeons in cities are treasured by pigeon fanciers who raise them for a variety of esoteric purposes. Other city pigeons are deemed pests because they deposit their droppings on buildings, and on handsome statues in parks. Barn pigeons are not always welcomed by farmers because they "mess up the hay." Wild, free-living pigeons tend to nest in cliff cavities along rivers. They are known as *rock doves* by bird watchers and ornithologists.

The city pigeons, the barn pigeons, and the rock doves all taste alike to me. Excellent, dark meat, but these birds fly around so much that their breasts tend to be tough. My favorite recipe follows:

SOUP ONE

1 pigeon
1 potato
1 onion
1 green pepper
(1 carrot)
(1 stalk celery)
Salt and pepper to taste

Dress the bird (see page 77), and boil it in lightly salted water until the bones are easily removed. Save broth and set meat aside. In the broth, boil 1 cut up potato, 1 sliced onion, and maybe 1 each of some other vegetables: carrot, stalk of celery, etc. When done — about 20–30 minutes — add meat, season to taste, and serve in bowls.

SQUAB

Squabs are young pigeons. They are the only milk-fed birds I've ever eaten, and I find them absolutely delicious. Until they leave the nest, their principal source of food is pigeon milk which the young get from their parents' mouths.

We usually find our squabs in barns — up in the hayloft. And we like to take the squabs shortly before they leave the nest, or when they just scurry away a few feet at your approach. At this age they actually tend to be *heavier* than the adults, as well as tender and fine-flavored.

Preheat oven. Roast 15 minutes at 350°.

WATERFOWL

Ducks

One's attitude toward the preparation of wildfowl for the table must be flexible. The quality of the bird is a more important consideration than the species among those ducks which are ordinarily considered good table ducks. It is possible to misjudge a duck but one can usually look a bird over carefully, sniff it, and decide whether it is a bird of merit to be dealt with as gently and simply as possible to bring out the full flavor, or whether it is a bird requiring very nice management to make it agreeable.

Schools of thought on cooking wildfowl tend to be violent and prejudiced, ranging from "fifteen minutes in a hot oven" to methods such as soakings and parboilings to get rid of "that wild taste." I doubt whether it is possible to become a good wildfowl cook as long as one adheres to either school of thought. Each has its place, but the range of most excellent wildfowl cooking lies between these two extremes.

Good eating ducks should be served rare (conceivably medium). Ducks should only be well done if there is something wrong with them.

Reputation of ducks

EXCELLENT FLAVOR	MIDDLING OR VARIABLE	POOR
Canvasback	Shoveller	Scoters
Mallard	Bluebills (scaups)	Oldsquaw
Black Duck	Ringnecks	Common Merganser
Blue-winged Teal	Goldeneye	
Green-winged Teal	Bufflehead	
Baldpate (wigeon)	Hooded Merganser	
Pintail		
Wood Duck		
Redhead		
Gadwall		

BREAST CONTOUR	SKIN COLOR	SMELL	GRADE
Pleasingly plump	Rich yellowish tan; fat under the breast skin	Clean, duck	Epicurean
Rather normal; a touch of yellow	A touch of yellow	Duck (pleasant)	Middling
The nadir of wretchedness	Dull, greyish; little or no fat	Fishy or rank	Parboil
	If you have brought home a duck with an unpleasant chemical odor (pollution taint), pluck the handsomest feather, and bury the duck.		Bury

This table should not be taken too seriously. Reputation is not always a guide to cookery. A mallard or a canvasback, for example, will taste no better than a scoter if its diet has been fishy, or the tribulations of a long and presumably arduous migration have reduced it to the nadir of wretchedness.

On the other hand individual hooded mergansers or shovellers may be so delicate and savory that all they need is judicious timing in a hot oven to rank them among the choicest ducks.

Age. Young grouse and young rabbits require less cooking than older individuals.

I have not found this to be the case with ducks. The Bursa of Fabricius technique described on page 71 enables one to tell birds of the year from older ducks. It won't help one with the problem of telling a year and a half old bird from an ancient.

Ageing or ripening. The old school duck hunters and gourmets argued about ageing. I used to hear these long arguments as a child and I wish now that I had paid more attention to them for the excellence of the ducks on our family table was extraordinary. Everyone was ordered out of the kitchen while Father cooked the ducks. I do not recall that anyone even suggested that it might be possible to eat a duck fresh-killed. Father would probably have failed to understand what the man was talking about.

The discussions usually ranged around how many weeks to hang a duck and whether it should be hung by its head or by its feet. Father hung his ducks undrawn and by the head . . . not till the tail feathers dropped out – that was too much . . . but until they came out at the slightest pull. He used to go into the back hall and tweak tail feathers, rather like testing a pineapple for ripeness.

His oven was hot, his timing was the perfect minimum, and visiting ladies, who looked askance at the blood on the platter and set out to take a mouthful just to be polite – ate every morsel.

Ducks, if they fall into the epicurean class by the Duck Judging Table, benefit by ageing. Four to ten days at 35 to 40 degrees is sufficient for most tastes, and those who cannot abide "high" meat ordinarily eat ten-day ducks with relish. A fresh-killed duck tastes very good, but the best ducks, in my opinion deserve at least four days of hanging. Fishy or gut-shot wildfowl should be dressed immediately and only the latter benefit by hanging.

Wildfowl recipes

ROAST DUCK, EPICUREAN

Pluck dry, dress and clean. Sprinkle with salt. Bake in a hot oven (450°). Good ducks should be served rare. Twenty minutes for a teal, 30 minutes for a mallard, 20–25 minutes for medium-sized ducks.

Roast duck is delicious cooked inside a wood heating stove. Use oak or hickory and let the fire die down until the flames are no longer leaping high. Fasten a wire through the duck and hang it neck downwards inside the stove out of reach of the flames.

ROAST DUCK, MIDDLING

Prepare and cook as above, but stuff with an apple or onion and increase the cooking time by one third. Ducks with an insufficient layer of fat should be basted with fat at intervals.

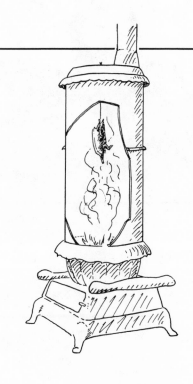

RAGOUT OF DUCK

Parboiling should only be used as a last resort for inferior wildfowl. The object is not to remove "that wild taste," but to disguise an unfortunate flavor. Ducks that look or smell as though they might require parboiling should be cleaned promptly. If they are fishy, they should be skinned, as fishy flavors emanate from the fat of the skin.

Duck
Vinegar
2 large onions
1 bunch carrots
4 potatoes
Bacon fat or salt pork
Salt and pepper

Soak one hour in cold water to which two tablespoons vinegar or two tablespoons soda per quart have been added. If the ducks are still fishy, parboil a half hour in salted water. Cut duck in pieces and place in a casserole dish with two large onions (sliced), 1 bunch carrots, 4 potatoes, and 4 tablespoons bacon fat or salt pork. Sprinkle with salt and pepper, add water to cover, and bake covered 1½ hours in a moderate oven (350°). (See also recipe for coot.)

It sometimes happens that one is in doubt as to whether or not the fat of a given duck will taste good. This subject can lead to very profitable discussions; however, if one prefers to settle the matter quickly, just cut off a small piece of fat, fry it, and eat it.

Wild goose

ROAST WILD GOOSE

These large birds are best roasted until well done, 30 minutes per pound at 325°. Do not stuff.

Serve with wild rice, fruit jelly, or applesauce.

Goose fat. This is first-rate shortening—good for cakes, pastry, and general cooking.

Coot

BAKED COOT

1 coot
Butter ½ the size of an egg
1 onion, sliced
Salt
Pepper
2 jiggers port

Skin, eviscerate, and wash in cold water. Place breast and legs in a casserole dish with butter ½ the size of an egg. Cover with a medium-sized onion (sliced). Sprinkle with salt and pepper. Add two jiggers of port. Bake 50 minutes in a hot (450°) oven.

Accompaniments for wildfowl

It has always been part of our hunting ethic to eat what we kill. Game in prime condition needs little to enhance it. For game of lesser quality, really good sauces make this ethic not too terribly hard to take.

For ducks epicurean. It is a desecration to diminish the flavor of a first-rate duck by pouring a sauce over it. Bread Sauce, however, is an excellent side dish.

BREAD SAUCE

2 onions, peeled and diced
Bacon fat
½ teaspoon allspice
¼ teaspoon cloves
½ teaspoon mace, thyme, or nutmeg
Salt and pepper to taste
Dry bread (about ¼ loaf)
Milk (about 1½ cups)

Fry onions in bacon fat, add spices, crumble bread over mixture and add just enough milk so that the whole is barely moistened. Heat and serve. Serves two. Enough for one medium-sized duck.

WILD RICE

See Wild Rice (page 81).

BROWN RICE

Same as Wild Rice. It may require 30 minutes of boiling.

For ducks middling. Middling ducks often benefit by a sauce or jelly.

CURRANT JELLY

Make like other jams and jellies (page 39).

CRANBERRY SAUCE

See Cranberries (page 88).

For ragout of duck (only). Some individuals—especially after a long migration, or having feasted on fish—are really not tasty, fit only for a ragout. A salad may be helpful.

Salads. Salads to be good should have a sharp piquant flavor and a fresh appreciable odor. A salad served with roast duck blunts one's taste so that the rich mellowness of the duck's flavor is lost.

It should no more occur to one to serve a salad with a first-rate duck dinner than to use moth balls for a centerpiece.

Wild cranberries

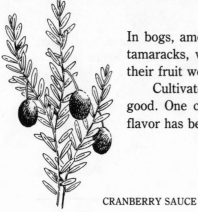

In bogs, among leatherleaf and sphagnum, and often near scattered tamaracks, wild cranberries fruit in the autumn, sometimes holding their fruit well into winter.

Cultivated cranberries are very like wild cranberries and fully as good. One cannot say as much for some cultivated fruits in which flavor has been sacrificed for looks and keeping qualities.

CRANBERRY SAUCE

2 cups sugar
2 cups water
6 cups cranberries

Bring to a good rolling boil and boil for ten minutes, stirring occasionally.

CRANBERRY COMPOTE
(Bavarian Style)

2 cups sugar
1 cup water
1 pound cranberries (about 1 quart)

Boil sugar and water to make a syrup. Cool slightly, so berries will not pop. Add cranberries and cook very slowly for two to eight hours. I set mine on the wood stove for a day.

Squirrel

Young squirrels, less than a year old, are tender. I know no easy way of distinguishing between young and old males, but the nipples of older females are apparent whereas those of the younger ones (which have not borne young) are very difficult to find. Select young animals for simple frying.

FRIED SQUIRREL

Add a little garlic salt to the fat before putting in the meat. Dip the meat into flour, salt, and fry until tender. About 15 to 20 minutes.

FOR OLDER SQUIRRELS

Proceed as above, then cover with water and bake in a slow oven.

STEWED SQUIRREL

1 squirrel
1 cup barley
1 onion

Cover with water (adding more as needed). Boil about an hour with onion and barley. Season to taste.

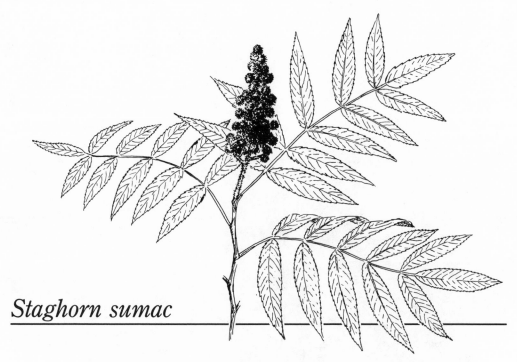

Staghorn sumac

Sumac not only has magnificent scarlet leaves in fall to put in vases—it has other attributes: Its hollow stems are perfect to use for drawing sap from sugar maples (but that is another story).

I have never known sumac to grow tall enough to interfere with utility wires—but it is often sprayed, lest it might. We do not recommend sumac lemonade spiked with herbicides.

SUMAC LEMONADE

Fill ⅓ of a glass of water with the dark red, velvety fruits of sumac. Squash them and drink an excellent lemonade. No sugar is needed.

It is easy to tell velvety red fruits from the hard little ball-type fruits of poison sumac. Leave those strictly for the birds.

There is a curious parallel that seems to have gone unnoticed. Those who feast on wild foods in spring, summer, and early autumn when it is warm, eat plenty of fruits and vegetables. And in winter, when it is cold, fruits and vegetables are scarce: our diets become more carnivorous. The geographic areas of the world are arranged in the same way. The closer to the tropics, the more fruits and vegetables are eaten; the closer to the poles, the more meat.

The ease of food storage and transportation has all but masked seasonal dietary differences. Quite inadvertently, the wild foods in this book, arranged by season, point up these differences. Meat is the main food of winter.

WINTER

Wild meats vary the menu enormously. I give instructions for preparing over forty wild meats. The meat for sale in most butcher shops comes from just a few species: cattle, pigs, chickens, and turkeys. Domestic ducks, geese, and sheep are far less commonly eaten, and lots of people have never even tasted goat. All these domestic animals stem from wild animals, so there isn't as sharp a line between wild and domestic as one might think. Some people think it right to eat only wild animals, and some feel equally strongly that only domestic animals should be eaten. I have been told, "They are *made* for that!" It is my hunch that the animals themselves are not aware of the distinction.

Be that as it may, wild animals are ordinarily eaten by hunters or catchers, and domestic animals are ordinarily eaten by people for whom the killing is done out of sight.

Those who would never consume a wild animal often feast happily on fish. Most fish are wild animals. A few, catfish for example, are becoming domesticated. Are catfish reared in pools happier than those grubbing about on muddy bottoms in the wild?

Sweet fern

The catkins, stem tips and dried leaves make a fragrant tea. Bring the water to a rolling boil, add a handful of sweet fern for a quart of tea, and boil a moment or two longer. Drink hot and soon, for the fragrance is ephemeral, and the taste scarcely perceptible.

Teas are a happy solution to the problem of some unsafe drinking water in camp. If dubious about the drinking water, boil it at least five minutes before making tea.

The sunflower group

Compass plant, cup plant, prairie dock, and sunflowers are closely related. Their seeds often contain little meat, but they are pleasant to munch. And they are available in late autumn, and even in early winter. The gummy juices of some of these plants—especially compass plant—are nice for chewing.

COMPASS PLANT

CUP PLANT

SUNFLOWER

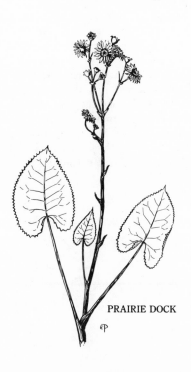

PRAIRIE DOCK

Venison or deer meat

Epicures speak of venison. Those who live in the brush, and whose families are apt to eat "a whole lot of beans," if the hunter fails, call it deer meat.

Be it venison, or deer meat, most of it is delicious and can be treated like any hunk of beef. That is easy. In this section I point the way to getting the most out of the flavor of *venison,* rather than beef. I also point the way to those many little problems that may arise when dealing with the meat of a large animal—let's face it—not *always* to be graded as "U.S. Choice."

Dressing out. Deer should be dressed out promptly and kept dry. *Do not wash,* or rub out with snow, except where the contents of paunch or intestines touch edible meat. Moisture encourages the very organisms that make meat spoil. Keep most of the meat about ten days at just above freezing. Some prefer much longer ageing, but the amount of once-good meat thrown away as a result of too long ageing is appalling. Liver, heart, brains, kidneys, and tongue need not be aged.

Keeping camp deer—or if your freezer is full. Leave the skin on. Increase the length of the incision that you made to dress the deer out. Loosen the skin until you can lift the carcass up by its "waist" and shove a small log between the backbone and the skin. Saw the deer in half, severing it between the ribs and the loin. The log was just to keep you from sawing into the skin. Remove it. Cut out the flanks and ribs and eat them soon, as they keep least well. Fold the flaps of skin back over the meat to protect it.

From now on, loosen the skin enough to take meat out as needed. The skin is a far better wrapper than waxed paper. It is clean, greased, handy, and has considerable insulating power as well. However, keep hair off the meat as much as possible. During a warm spell, keep the meat well wrapped by day, but open the flaps wide at night. The skin will protect the meat from freezing hard during short cold snaps. This system does not waste the skin; one can tan it after one has finished up the venison.

Alternate freezing and thawing. Wide variations in temperature are not desirable for keeping meat. Disdaining meat that has been subjected to alternate freezing and thawing need not, however, become a fetish.

View with suspicion any meat that has had a chance to *spoil.* Remember, meat once frozen (or washed) spoils more quickly than meat which has been allowed to dry naturally. I have found that meat that has gotten the frost into it and thawed out off and on, without, however, getting a chance to spoil, is often delicious and almost invariably has improved in texture.

Warm weather. Deer killed in weather so warm that the meat will not cool in a matter of hours present a real test of skill. Such meat not only needs to be dressed out promptly, but also should be skinned without delay. It won't cool down fast enough to prevent spoilage with the skin on. Guard this meat from flies and from moisture. A good emergency method for holding such meat in camp is to hang chunks out at night, high above dogs or coyotes. Then wrap it in canvas and quilts early each morning, to keep it cool during the heat of the day.

A big cooked roast keeps a lot longer than a pile of fresh steaks.

How to tell the age of a deer. Many hunters, woodsmen, and even camp cooks think they know exactly how to tell the age of a deer. "Look at that big rack!" they exclaim. "It's got to be the granddaddy of them all." And they are so wrong. In the Lake States deer antlers are not much help in telling a deer's age. Large, fine antlers do not necessarily mean an old deer. Heavy antlers, with five or six points on each side, and magnificent spread, are often found on young (3½-year-old) white-tailed deer. Even year-and-a-half old deer may also have several points on each side. Old deer (7 to 10 years, or more) may have very few points. Spike bucks in the hunting season are usually a year-and-a-half old, and button bucks, with antlers not quite erupted, are fawns.

The diameter of the antler tends to increase with age, but there is considerable variation.

Age can be determined with a high degree of accuracy by examining the teeth. A few very worn teeth, however, do not mean that the deer is old. It is customary to examine the lower jaw. If the first three grinding teeth are badly worn, but the rest still carry high crests, the deer is a youngster about to shed its baby teeth at 18 months. If it only has four grinders it is a fawn. If all its grinding teeth (premolars and molars) show really heavy wear, it is an ancient.

Dental age characters of white-tailed deer (cheek side of lower molar row). This ageing technique was developed by C. W. Severinghaus; the drawings were prepared by the Missouri Conservation Commission.

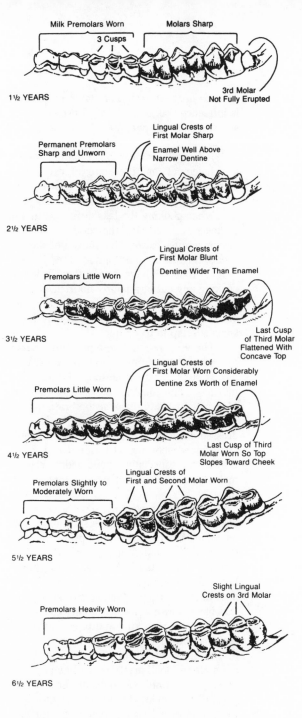

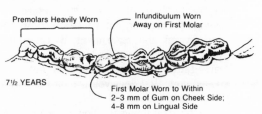

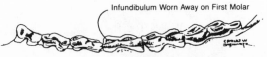

How to judge a deer. The flavor of venison is influenced sometimes by its browse, sometimes by its age, and always by the cook.

Judging deer meat is not simple. There are choice cuts and there are inferior cuts. But consider, as well, there are choice animals and there are inferior animals.

When cooking the less desirable cuts of a choice, well-fed deer the cook is circumventing *texture:* the bottom of the round, the shank, and the neck tend to be tougher (but still have a good flavor). When cooking any cut of a poorly nourished, or starving deer, the cook is circumventing not only texture, but *flavor* as well! There is some overlap in techniques.

There is nothing like a pressure cooker to tenderize tough meat, and convert it into a tasty stew. There is nothing like the judicious—and sometimes extravagant—use of strong spices to mask second-rate flavor.

Because it has such a rangy build, a dressed out deer is apt to look thin. Do not be deceived; look for fat inside. Good browse and especially a good acorn crop make for a nice layer of fat and superlative meat.

At the other extreme, pink or coral-colored bone marrow means starvation. Not only does this condition pose problems for the cook—demanding many variations of stews and ragouts till the deer is eaten up—but it also raises questions for the naturalist. Deer and man are two species that have shown a marked ability to over-produce their own kind and to so destroy their habitat that they can no longer live in it. The yards where the marrow-pink deer are gathered look pretty much like any other woods, until one looks closely.

For the novice there is one comforting thought in deer judging. Just as the girl in the beauty shop takes a test curl before giving a permanent, cut a test steak, or even several, and experiment. By the time you have cooked your first quail you've learned little, but by the time you have cooked your first deer you are on the way to becoming an expert.

After examining the bone marrow, take a tiny chunk of fat and heat it over a

candle. Then taste it. If it tastes good, use it in cooking. Most deer fat tastes terrible, so let your stews cool till the fat hardens and skim it off. Make soap or another candle, but don't spoil the taste of your dinner. Use the fat of the pig to make your venison cookery delicious.

Try the first test steaks rare and only increase the cooking time if necessary.

If the meat is higher than you like it, probably only the outside is over-ripe. If simply dry and dark, trim it off and read the recipe for dried venison. If moist and odoriferous, cut off and discard the outside. If merely dubious, boil for about five minutes in water to which one tablespoon soda per quart has been added, and roast as usual. Mildew should be wiped off or cut away.

Deerslayer Pussyfoot Paulson's method of making deer antler buttons.

1. To make deer antler buttons, I choose a sound antler, preferably from a buck I have adroitly stalked and shot. Freshly dropped antlers will do, but ones that have been weathering on the ground for a season or two are usually too porous and soft for buttons. If you want to make buttons from the bucks that you shoot, shoot ones with button-sized racks. Don't shoot bucks with trophy racks! It's very difficult, if not impossible, to cut up trophy racks. Ego always seems to get in the way. Can't brag about that trophy via buttons on a sweater.

2. On a cold winter day, by a crackling fire, I like to make my antler buttons with the following tools:

Small fine-toothed metal cutting
handsaw, such as a hacksaw;

Large (about 14 inch) bastard file;
Small to medium (6–10 inch) size *mill*
  bastard file. This file will make
  smoother surfaces than the larger-
  toothed bastard;
Hand drill with a ¹/₁₆ inch steel drill bit;
¼ inch steel drill bit;
Pocket knife.

3. I saw off the antler at the point where the diameter is beginning to be the size of the buttons I want. I progressively cut off the buttons towards the base of the antler. When sawing through the antler, I keep an even, smooth pressure on the saw. This reduces the chance of an uneven and ragged cut.

4. The freshly sawed antler is fairly rough. It is easier to smooth the exposed end while it is still part of the antler. I smooth it first with the large bastard file and finish the smoothing process with the smaller mill bastard file.

5. Next I saw off a button from the end of the antler. It should be at least ⅛-inch thick. I make a concentrated effort to keep an even thickness.

6. I smooth this freshly cut end of the button with both the large and smaller files.

I find holding down on the button with my fingers and pulling the button over the files much easier than pushing the files over a stationary button.

7. With a hand drill and a ¹/₁₆ inch steel drill bit, I drill two holes into the smoothed-off button. I make sure the distance between these holes is at least two hole diameters (⅛ inch) apart. As the button diameter gets larger I make this distance greater. The space between the holes is necessary to keep the center of the button from wearing out.

8. With my fingers, I gently rotate a ¼-inch steel drill bit in the button's holes. I do it just enough to round off the sharp edges that the smaller drill bit has made and thus extend the life of the button's thread.

9. The finishing touch on the button is a careful inspection. With the finer-toothed file or a pocket knife, I gently smooth off any rough edges that remain so they won't snag or flake off during use.

10. I could use appropriate power tools to make antler buttons, but the noise, speed and vibrations interfere with the nostalgia of past experiences and dreams of future hunts.

—Dale Paulson

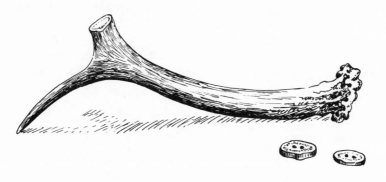

How to eat up a whole deer

These recipes are grouped primarily in order of choiceness. To be practical and not waste meat eat the deer up in the order of perishability: lungs, flank, ribs, brain, tongue, neck, shanks—and *then,* chops, steaks, and roasts.

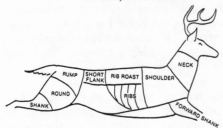

Choice cuts. The best cuts of venison are easy to prepare and require less cooking. Epicures prefer venison roasts, steaks, and chops rare. In general, venison is cooked like beef. First-rate venison is choicest rare: 20 minutes per pound with the oven at 300°, or broiled.

ROAST VENISON

Cover with strips of salt pork or bacon. Start roast in preheated oven.

Rare	20 minutes per pound at 300° F.
Medium	22–25 minutes per pound at 300° F.
Well done	27–30 minutes per pound at 300° F.

To brown, raise the oven temperature the last 15 minutes.

Serve with fruit jelly.

CHOPS AND STEAKS

Broil or fry. Serve with mushrooms.

CHUCK ROAST

Take out the bone. Scatter thick slices of ham fat or bacon through the roast in the cuts already made, and cover the top of the roast with strips of bacon.

Tie the roast with string, rolling in any odd flaps of meat to make a neat bundle.

Heat about ¼ cup bacon fat in the roaster and sear the roast on all sides. Salt lightly and surround with one large sliced onion. Roast 30 minutes per pound at 350°.

Put the roast in the warming oven while making the gravy, which should be made in the roaster.

VENISON GRAVY

¼ cup sliced ham fat or bacon
Flour to thicken (about 2 tablespoons)
Hot water, 1 to 2 cups
Bouillon cubes
1 large onion
Sweet red wine to taste

Stir the flour into the hot fat and juices in the roaster. Add hot water gradually (one to two cups). Season with one or two bouillon cubes. Just before serving, when the gravy is all made, is the moment to add the sweet red wine.

How to cook orts (overlooked delicacies).
With the present price of meat I shall dwell on orts (the parts that are usually thrown to the dogs) and how to recognize and not waste delectable trifles.

FRIED KIDNEYS

Deer kidneys are delicious simply split lengthwise, and fried. It seems a pity that they are so small—and each deer has but two.

KIDNEYS OF THE HUNT BREAKFAST
(Dr. Wolf Dietsche)

For many years it has been a tradition that, after the long days of the deer hunt, friends gather at the Jagdschloss to swap stories— and to eat. There is always a special dish for breakfast. Preparation starts the evening before. Cut out each renal pelvis (the white, fatty area in each kidney). Slice each kidney in small slices, much as you would slice a banana. Wash the slices in three waters, drain them, and set them aside in a cool place.

4 kidneys
4 slices of bacon
1 onion (chopped fine)
4 capfuls of red vermouth (1 per kidney)

Fry the bacon, add onion and sauté until golden brown. Add a capful of red (sweet) vermouth per kidney and sauté the kidneys 3 to 5 minutes. You can see them turn color when done.

DEER BRAINS

Separate the head from the neck by cutting to the base of the skull all the way round and then wringing the head off with a quick twist. Pull the brains out with a small ice tea spoon.

Scramble with one or two eggs, 1/8 cup sherry and 1 tablespoon butter. Salt to taste. Serve hot with bacon.

DEER HEART

Either slice and cook like steak, or pressure cook 15 to 20 minutes at 15 pounds and serve with deer tongue sauce.

DEER TONGUE

Boil in salted water until the skin peels off easily. Serve with deer tongue sauce. (See page 102.)

DEER LIVER

Slice very thin (1/2 inch) with a sharp knife. Fry quickly in fat hot enough so the liver sizzles the moment it touches the fat. Do not heat the fat to the smoking point. Liver gets tough with long cooking.

Livers of some deer benefit by parboiling. Slice thin, drop into boiling water and boil two minutes, then fry until nicely browned. Salt just before serving.

Livers of deer are not always good to eat. They may be so tough and rank that they may not even make a good pâté.

VENISON LIVER PÂTÉ

2 pounds liver
3/4 pound butter or shortening
2 onions
1 teaspoon allspice
1/2 teaspoon thyme
Salt and pepper

Slice and sauté the liver. Chop liver and onions very fine, the finer the better. Season with spices, salt and pepper.

Cook at 15 pounds pressure for 40 minutes.

LUNG SOUP

Fry two large onions in lard or bacon fat until golden brown. Meanwhile cut the lungs into 1-inch cubes. Add to the simmering onions together with potatoes, celery, carrots, leftover salad. Cook until the potatoes are done. Do *not* salt. Add chicken or beef bouillon cubes instead. A ham bone cooked with the soup improves the flavor.

At best, lung soup is hardly a gourmet dish. But if one wants to eat the whole deer, even the lungs can be made edible.

Trimmings and scraps. The less desirable cuts and the trimmings still have their place. Ribs, flank, shank, neck, and sometimes shoulder (chuck) are often best used as hamburger, borsch, stew, mincemeat, sausage, and the like.

VENISON BORSCH

1 pound meat (less tender cuts will do)
2 cups chopped cabbage
1 large onion, peeled and chopped
1 can beets (about ½ pint)
3 tablespoons vinegar or lemon
Spiced salt or bouillon cubes
Salt and pepper
½ pint sour cream

Cut meat into stew-sized chunks. Cover with salted water and boil until tender. Add two cups chopped cabbage, one finely cut onion, and cook until cabbage is done. Add three tablespoons of vinegar or lemon juice. Season with pepper and spiced salt or bouillon cubes. Serve hot with cold sour cream on top.

Left-over borsch, heated up the next day, tastes even better than the first time.

This is merely a soup. Sradnaj Rossiaj borsch, on the other hand, is a feast, and may be served as a main course.

SRADNAJ ROSSIAJ BORSCH
(Alina Scharko)

2 pounds deer meat (stew cuts)
1 soup bone (not just ribs)
1 carrot, cut up
2 potatoes, diced
1 cup diced canned beets (or fresh)
2 cups sliced cabbage
⅛ pound salt pork (preferably aged)
1 onion, sliced
1 cup canned tomatoes
Vinegar or lemon
1 pint sour cream
1 small piece of sharp red pepper
Boletus or other mushrooms optional

Meat of members of the deer family, beef, or lean pork are suitable for borsch. One should never use young animals as they are too weak in flavor. It is customary to save up a chunk of salt pork for a year or so, cutting off little pieces as needed. For borsch-making, salt pork improves in flavor as it turns yellowish with age. A little bacon rind, added to the borsch, gives a good flavor and is a fair substitute for properly aged salt pork.

Cover the meat and soup bone with salted water to which a finely cut carrot and two diced potatoes have been added. (If fresh beets are to be used, dice them and put them into the soup pot now.) Cook about an hour. Take the meat out when it is done. Add canned beets including the liquid, two cups of sliced cabbage, and a tiny piece of sharp red pepper.

Try out the salt pork in a frying pan and fry a sliced onion until browned. Empty the contents of the frying pan into the soup. When the cabbage is done, add one cup of canned tomatoes and put the meat in again.

Now is the time to taste the borsch, which should have a slightly tart or sour taste. If not sour enough, add a little vinegar or lemon juice; if too sour, add a little sugar. The tartness of the borsch should come into a nice balance with the smoothness of the sour cream, which I prefer to serve separately. People can help themselves to as much as they want.

VENISON CURRY

½ pound bacon or salt pork (cubed)
1 pound onions (sliced)
4 cloves garlic (minced)
1 teaspoon turmeric
1 teaspoon ginger
1 teaspoon paprika
1 teaspoon cumin
2 teaspoons coriander
2 teaspoons chili
2 or 3 pounds venison (cut in bite-sized pieces)
2 or 3 cups yogurt   Salt to taste

Fry bacon or salt pork till crisp. Add sliced onions and venison and sauté until onions are golden brown. Add yogurt. Cover and simmer until meat is tender. If in a hurry, start the recipe in a pressure cooker and, instead of simmering the ingredients, process 40 minutes at 20 pounds pressure.

VENISON SCRAPPLE

After skinning out a deer, those hunters who take pride in caring for the meat usually walk around the carcass. They are sizing up where they will make their cuts for steaks, chops, roasts. Often they wonder how they will get it all into the freezer. How to "condense" the bony parts of a deer so that no meat goes to waste?

Long years ago the Pennsylvania Dutch solved this problem with the pig. They were thrifty folk and no edible part of the pig went to waste. The cheaper cuts were made into scrapple: a delicacy that many rate higher than a good pork roast. Venison scrapple is likewise excellent.

DARK PARTS ARE SCRAPPLE MEAT.

Place a large container beside you before you start to cut up your deer (a 16-quart pressure cooker is ideal, but a big bucket will do).

Cut off the feet for a gun rack or use them in the backyard to teach children how to recognize deer tracks.

Plan your next cuts as high up the legs as you want to. There is very little meat on the lower portion of the legs, but there is some and there is lots of good bone. The broth from cooked bones makes scrapple hang together. Remove any meat you want to save for hamburger. If you prefer to make lots of scrapple, add the leg bones *and* meat to the scrapple pot.

Next, saw off the ribs and add them with the flanks to the pot; add the tail. Cut and package the choice cuts. The neck is bony and takes up lots of freezer space—into the scrapple pot. Some add the head too (it is customary to remove the eyes first).

Deer meat *and* bones

Cornmeal—not more than ⅔ cup per pound of meat

Bacon or ham with some fat—1/32 pound per pound of meat

Onion—one medium-sized onion per pound of meat

Thyme, sage, or both

Oregano

Salt

Garlic

Scrapple is made in two stages: first cook in salted water until the meat falls from the bones. Pressure cookers save a lot of time. Cool enough so you can remove the bones. Skim off any fat. Put ¼ cup of the remaining liquid in the refrigerator to cool (trust me, explanation later).

Estimate the weight of the *meat* (not including the liquid). The flavor of pig is essential to good scrapple. One *eighth* of a pound of bacon or ham (with some fat) is enough to flavor 4 pounds of deer meat. Add a medium-sized onion per pound of meat. Season lightly with thyme or sage or both and add oregano, salt, and a little garlic.

Did the ¼ cup of liquid turn into jelly? If not, keep the big pot boiling and keep cooling samples until one sample passes the jelly test. Then add cornmeal gradually and not more than ⅔ cup per pound of meat. Keep stirring (the bottom is apt to catch), keep tasting and add seasoning to taste.

Most recipes omit the jelly test and recommend cooking over low heat for an hour after the cornmeal has been added. I cut the time to 10 minutes and stir vigorously.

Pack the scrapple in small containers and store chilled or frozen. To serve, slice ½ inch thick and fry in bacon fat until there is a crisp and brown crust. Some say the crust is the best part.

Scrapple is delicious with the breakfast eggs, nice for a luncheon party, and a mercy when dinner guests arrive unannounced.

VENISON MINCEMEAT

1 quart canned blueberries
1 cup cranberry sauce
½ pound ground deer meat
¼ cup sugar
¼ cup fat (goose fat, chicken fat or butter—not deer fat!)
½ cup raisins
2 tablespoons molasses
½ teaspoon cinnamon
½ teaspoon clove
½ teaspoon nutmeg
Brandy
Salt

Fry meat in fat. Pour off and set aside the blueberry juice. Combine the ingredients (except the brandy). Add enough blueberry juice to keep the mixture moist. Bring to a rolling boil, and then reduce heat and cook slowly for at least ½ hour. Keep adding blueberry juice as required. Taste the mincemeat, flavor with brandy (brandy extract will do), add salt, and more sugar, or spices to suit your taste.

Substitutions: if fresh cranberries are used, add extra sugar. Apples may be used in place of blueberries, but if they are not very tart, add lemon, currant jelly or wild cherry jelly.

Mincemeat should contain some juice when it is put into the pie. Mince pies are particularly apt to boil over while baking. Seal the edges of the pastry carefully. Poke depressions in the upper crust with a hole at the bottom of each; juices may properly escape from these.

Sauces for venison

DEER TONGUE SAUCE

½ cup brown sugar
1 tablespoon flour
1 cup raisins (yellow raisins are especially nice)
Salt to taste
⅛ cup garlic flavored red wine vinegar
¾ cup water

Mix dry ingredients, add liquids and cook to a syrup. Serve hot poured over the meat.

FATHER'S SAUCE

½ pound salt pork
1 16-ounce can cranberry sauce
1 10½-ounce can condensed tomato soup
1 1-ounce jar currant or wild cherry jelly
5 ounce (½ can) consommé or bouillon
Salt, pepper, and paprika

Slice the salt pork about ½ inch thick and cut deeply along the edge of each slice to prevent curling while frying.

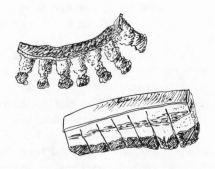

Combine ingredients and bring to a boil. Put chunks of meat into the hot sauce and cook until tender.

Dried venison

UNSPICED DRIED VENISON

Cut meat into thin strips and let hang well above a slow fire until hard.

Under some circumstances, for example, bright sunlight in the broiling desert, meat dries well without a fire.

JERKY
(Keith Janick)

Spice fresh meat with:

3 pounds salt

4 tablespoons allspice

5 tablespoons black pepper (preferably freshly ground)

Cut meat into 1 × 1 × 6 inch strips. Roll in spices. Hang in wood stove overnight (on an old coat hanger).

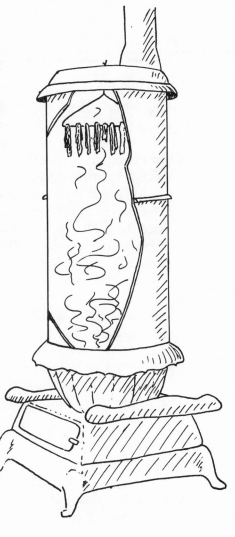

Cottontails, jackrabbits and snowshoe hares

In general, cook the big old ones like an old stewing hen, but treat the young ones like chicken.

These animals may have warbles in the skin, warty hornlike growths on the skin, or internal cysts. These may be cut away. Discard them, but not the rabbit.

My friend Arnold Haugen said that the psychic effect on a hunter of the presence of heavy infestations of parasites on rabbits is of importance. Probably many a rabbit has been discarded because of its unsightly appearance due to the presence of warbles, papillomas, or cysticerci. Do not toss the discarded cysts to your dog as they are probably the larvae of the dog tapeworm. It's like *giving* him tapeworms!

Small spots on both spleen and liver are serious. They indicate Tularemia or rabbit fever, a nasty disease occasionally fatal to man. Cooked, the rabbit is safe. Raw, it is not even safe to touch him. Rubber gloves are said to give a measure of protection. Local outbreaks of Tularemia usually receive considerable publicity. Incidence of Tularemia is said to decrease after severe frost.

FRIED RABBIT

Clean and cut the rabbit into about six pieces for frying. Dip in flour, and fry in hot but not smoking bacon fat. Add two or three sliced onions, and salt well.

After the meat is well browned, turn the heat low and finish cooking with a cover on the pan, or finish it off in the oven (350°).

It takes 30 minutes for a full grown but not old cottontail.

Most cottontails are less than 12 months old. If, after 15 minutes of cooking, it is not easy to plunge a fork into the meat, one needs to modify this recipe. If in a hurry, empty the contents of the frying pan into a pressure cooker, add 1 cup water, and process 30 minutes at 15 pounds. If not in a hurry, add a little water and finish cooking in the oven. This will take about 45 to 60 minutes.

HASENPFEFFER

1 rabbit, cut up
1 cup vinegar
½ teaspoon thyme
½ teaspoon basil
½ teaspoon allspice
Pepper and salt
1 onion
1 cup sour cream

Cut the rabbit up as for frying. Mix a brine of equal parts of vinegar and water (2 cups of brine for one cottontail); spices and onion. Soak meat in brine for 36 hours. Then remove meat, dry it, and brown it in fat. Add the onion, one cup of brine and one cup sour cream. Simmer 20 minutes and season to taste.

Use rabbits or hares, young or old.

RABBIT SOUP

1 can black bean soup
1 can consomme
½ cup water
2 cups cooked rabbit meat
4 tablespoons sherry
1 hard boiled egg

Combine and heat the first four ingredients. Just before serving add four tablespoons sherry and garnish with sliced hard boiled egg.

Cattail

Muskrats eat cattail. People can, too. It is one of the most substantial of the wild winter vegetables. However, chopping the icebound roots and stem bases out of a marsh is hard work. And one would probably never go to the trouble to do this, preferring the comfortable knowledge that there is food underfoot in a cattail marsh if one really wanted it.

AS A SOUP THICKENER

Wash and peel the roots and stem bases. Slice lengthwise to expose the pith. Boil about 5 minutes. Scrape the pith out of the larger roots and strain the stringy portions out. The residue has a pleasant starchy taste and a texture not unlike tapioca.

AS A VEGETABLE

In winter, even moderately good vegetables are few in the northern states. Wash stem bases and cut longitudinally. Boil 20 minutes. The pulp has a faint sweet potato taste, and although it is stringy, it is good – even without salt.

In late spring or early summer, when the young "tails" have not quite peeped out of the upper leaves, they taste like zucchini squash, but are more juicy and mucilaginous. Boil 15 minutes and serve as a vegetable or add to chop suey. One can gather enough for a serving in a few minutes.

It is hard to starve in a marsh.

Muskrat

Duck hunting had been good down on the Mississippi Delta, but we wanted to bring our ducks back home. Privat's wife offered to cook us something else; so for the first time in our lives we feasted on "Marsh Hare"—of all things *muskrat*!

We have eaten many since then. Our trapper friends who always used to throw the meat to their dogs sometimes bring us carcasses. Some trappers enjoy the meat, too.

Muskrat should be dressed out promptly. However, if the pelt is to be saved, skin it first and then dress it out. Remove the musk glands which are small bodies on the inside of the thigh. Cook muskrat like rabbit or squirrel.

Muskrat is delicious.

"MARSH HARE" AUX CHAMPIGNONS

1 muskrat
1 can condensed mushroom soup
1 small onion
Salt and pepper

Quarter and sauté the meat with a small amount of sliced onion. (If not tender when cooked through, add water and simmer till tender.) Add one can condensed mushroom soup, season with salt and pepper, and stir until hot (not boiling).

FRIED MUSKRAT

Or your guests may prefer one of two recipes from Clarence Searles:

(1) Quarter the muskrat. Parboil with celery and onion for 20 minutes. Drain the meat, dredge with flour, and fry in bacon fat.

(2) Fry the meat like chicken, then cover the pot and bake for 1 hour in an oven at 350°.

Beaver

Beaver meat is a luxury. For some mysterious reason this is not well known. Perhaps it is the money value of the fur which lessens the prestige of the steak. Some trappers are epicures and it is plain that they and their friends, rather than city people, are the ones to consume this delicacy.

Beavers, like rabbits, may carry Tularemia, and the same precautions (examining the liver and spleen for spots) should be used while dressing them out and before eating.

BROILED BEAVER

Slice about an inch thick. Broil like a medium steak, turning once. Beavers are the only rodents which I find taste considerably better somewhat rare.

FRIED BEAVER
(Bill Boose)

Cut into about inch-square chunks so the meat can be easily stirred in the spider. (A spider is a black cast iron frying pan. Technically, only the ones with 5 legs were known as spiders.) Fry in butter, adding a medium-sized onion to a spiderful. Frying too long toughens the meat.

> The beaver's rather like a mouse
> It builds its house down by the shore
> Instead of in my bureau drawer.
> We trap them both and is their pain
> Wholly different? Just the same?

Porcupine

In some respects our northern states are still part of the wild, romantic frontier. There are big woods, and winter travel there is not for novices.

The Indians used to fear big woods, for game is scarce. They once fought for the edge between the big woods and the prairie where game was abundant, but I never heard tell of their fighting for any part of the big woods. Even bear and deer and ruffed grouse do far better where there are sizeable openings.

But the porcupine is scattered here and there throughout our northwoods. It is the only sizeable animal that just about anybody can kill with a club or stick.

A porcupine could save your life. None ever saved mine, but once, on an expedition in the Northwest Territories of Canada, we found a road-killed porcupine when meat was mighty welcome.

There is a difference between being hungry and having an appetite. If you only have an appetite, press on to some eating place, for porcupine may strike you as too fat and greasy. But if you are caught in the North, hungry and without food, not only the meat, but even the fat will taste just wonderful and be just what your body needs. Fat hunger is said to be one of the terrible hungers of the North.

Porcupines are not exceptionally difficult to skin out—even with a dull jackknife and a pair of pliers. A dead porcupine does not seem nearly as spiny as a live one. There are no spines in the way while making the ventral incision. Pliers are handy for pulling the skin away from the meat. They are handy too, if you've been unlucky enough to get porcupine quills under your own skin.

I've pulled quills from dogs and from hawks that have tangled with porcupines and even out of myself. To pull them out *twist* them as though each quill was a screw. They come out more smoothly and hurt less.

There must be many excellent ways of cooking porcupine. Especially where porcupines are being killed to protect timber from their girdling, culinary experiments could well produce results better than my own recipe.

BOILED PORCUPINE

Boil in salted water until tender. The meat is mild and pleasant.

Raccoon

Raccoon, like pork, should be thoroughly cooked, and for the same reason. It may contain Trichinae, and trichinosis is a singularly unpleasant disease to acquire. The intestines (and droppings) of raccoons often contain *Baylisascaris procyonis*. This is a round worm. It is the eggs that are usually ingested by people. Look out for the intestines! If the meat has been contaminated by contents of the intestine, we advise not eating the meat of that individual. At any rate, cook raccoons thoroughly.

ROASTED RACCOON
(Mary Mattson)

Vinegar
Carrots
Onions
Apple

Remove as much fat as can be stripped off before roasting. Also remove the scent glands; these kernel-like objects are set rather deeply under the forelegs, and at the tail base. It is absolutely necessary to remove the scent glands to avoid ruining the meat completely.

Wash coon well with vinegar water. Start in a slow oven, draining fat off frequently. Put raw carrots and onions and one apple inside the coon during the first part of roasting. When most of the fat has been taken care of by draining, remove the coon from the oven and take out the vegetables and dispose of them. Stuff the coon with standard sage dressing and return it to the oven. Roast at about 375°, timing as for pork (about 35 minutes per pound).

Avoid serving oily or greasy foods with a coon dinner. Good accompaniments are: baked potatoes, creamed cauliflower, buttered whole onions, corn custard loaf, spiced beets, and light fluffy desserts.

Opossum

The meat of these slow-moving mammals tastes rather like pork and "possum, pone, and sweet potato" is held in high esteem by many in the South. Some like their possums really fat and even hold them in pens to fatten them up for a feast.

Others consider the fat "greasy" and dispose of as much as possible of it before cooking. Possum meat is not especially popular in the northern states.

It is no trouble to distinguish between young and old possums at the northern limit of their range. *All* possums old enough to have lived through a winter got their tail tips frozen off; only the youngsters have gracefully pointed tips on their waving prehensile tails.

Roast like pork.

Mulligan

MULLIGAN STEW

This recipe is the great catch-all for hunters and trappers in the North—and fit for a queen.

Rabbits, pheasant, squirrel, crow, duck, etc.
Vegetables: carrots, beans, potatoes, toma-
  toes, etc.
Onions, fat, salt.

Fry onions in a big pot. Cut meat into pieces and brown in the same pot. Add vegetables, cover with salted water and bring to a boil. Then simmer for two or more hours.

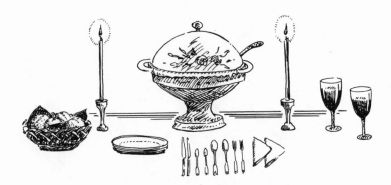

We used to keep a bucket of frozen mulligan hanging in the woodshed, chipping off chunks with an axe as needed.

Most of the Latin names were taken from the following sources, which are listed in the Bibliography.

Flowering plants: Fernald (1950);

Mushrooms: McKnight and McKnight (1987);

Amphibians and reptiles: Vogt (1981);

Fishes: Becker (1983);

Mammals: Nowak and Paradiso (1983);

Birds: American Ornithologists' Union (1983).

LIST OF LATIN NAMES

PLANTS

Acorn	*Quercus* spp.
Alfalfa	*Medicago sativa*
Artichoke, Jerusalem	*See* Jerusalem Artichoke
Aster	*Aster* spp.
Basswood	*Tilia americana*
Blackberry	*Rubus* spp. (subgenus *Eubati*)
Blueberry	*Vaccinium* spp.
Box elder	*Acer negundo*
Bracken	*Pteridium aquilinum*
Buckwheat	*Fagopyrum sagittatum*
Bugleweed	*Lycopus uniflorus*
Burdock	*Arctium minus*
Cattail	*Typha* spp.
Cherry, Black	*Prunus serotina*
Cherry, Choke	*Prunus virginiana*
Cherry, Pin	*Prunus pennsylvanica*
Clover, White	*Trifolium repens*
Compass-plant	*Silphium laciniatum*
Cowslip	*See* Marigold, Marsh
Cranberry, Highbush	*Viburnum trilobum*
Cranberry, Wild	*Vaccinium macrocarpon*
	Vaccinium oxycoccus
Cress, Water	*Nasturtium officinale*
Cup-plant	*Silphium perfoliatum*
Currant, Red	*Ribes sativum*
Dandelion	*Taraxacum officinale*
Dock, Prairie	*Silphium terebinthinaceum*
Dogbane	*Apocynaceae*
Elder, Common	*Sambucus canadensis*
Elderberry	*See* Elder, Common
Fern, Bracken	*See* Bracken
Fiddleheads	*See* Bracken
Fireweed	*Epilobium* spp.
Grape, Wild	*Vitis* spp.

113

Ground-cherry	*Physalis* spp.
Hemlock, Poison	*Conium maculatum*
Hemlock, Water	*Cicuta maculata*
Hog-peanut	*Amphicarpa bracteata*
Huckleberry	*Gaylussacia baccata*
Jerusalem Artichoke	*Helianthus tuberosus*
Juneberry	*Amelanchier* spp.
Lamb's-quarters	*Chenopodium album*
Mallow	*Malva neglecta*
Mandrake	*See* May-apple
Maple, Red or Soft	*Acer rubrum*
Maple, Silver or Soft	*Acer saccharinum*
Maple, Sugar	*Acer saccharum*
Marigold, Marsh	*Caltha palustris*
May-apple	*Podophyllum peltatum*
Mesquite	*Prosopis glandulosa*
Milkweed, Common	*Asclepias syriaca*
Mustard, Black	*Brassica nigra*
Mustard, White	*Brassica hirta*
Nannyberry	*Viburnum lentago*
Nettle, Stinging	*Urtica dioica*
Nightshade, Bittersweet	*Solanum dulcamara*
Nightshade, Black	*Solanum nigrum*
Nightshade, Deadly	*Solanum belladona*
Oak, Black	*Quercus velutina*
Oak, Bur	*Quercus macrocarpa*
Oak, Jack	*Quercus ellipsoidalis*
Oak, Red	*Quercus rubra*
Oak, White	*Quercus alba*
Parsley family	Umbelliferae
Parsnip, Water	*Berula pusilla*
Pigweed	*See* Lamb's-quarters
Plum, Wild	*Prunus americana*
Pusley	*Portulaca oleracea*
Raspberry	*Rubus idaeus*
Raspberry, Black	*Rubus occidentalis*
Rice, Wild	*Zizania aquatica*
Rose	*Rosa* spp.
Sage	*Artemesia* spp.
Shadbush	*See* Juneberry
Sheep-sorrel	*Rumex acetosella*
Sorrel, Wood	*Oxalis* spp.
Spanish-needles	*Bidens* spp.
Spurge	Euphorbiaceae
Strawberry	*Fragaria* spp.
Sumac, Poison	*Rhus vernix*
Sumac, Staghorn	*Rhus typhina*

Sunflower	*Helianthus annuus*
Sweet-fern	*Comptonia peregrina*
Thimbleberry	*Rubus parviflorus*
Tomatillo	*Physalis ixocarpa*
Violet	*Viola* spp.
Wood-sorrel	*Oxalis* spp.

MUSHROOMS

Amanita	*Amanita* spp.
Boletus	*Boletus* spp.
Chanterelle	*Cantharellus cibarius*
Destroying angel	*Amanita virosa*
Edible boletus	*Boletus edulis*
Elm mushroom	*See* Oyster mushroom
Fairy ring	*Marasmius oreades*
Honey cap	*Armillaria mellea*
Honey mushroom	See Honey cap
Morel	*Morchella* spp.
Morel, False	*Gyromitra* spp.
Oyster mushroom	*Pleurotus ostreatus*
Polypore, Sulphur	*See* Sulphur polypore
Puffball	*Calvatia gigantea*
	Lycoperdon perlatum
	Lycoperdon pyriforma
Shaggymane	*Coprinus comatus*
Shoestring mushroom	*See* Honey cap
Sulphur polypore	*Polyporus sulphureus*

ANIMALS

INVERTEBRATES

Crayfish	*Cambarus* spp.

AMPHIBIANS

Bullfrog	*Rana catesbeiana*
Green frog	*Rana clamitans*
Leopard frog	*Rana pipiens*
Wood frog	*Rana sylvatica*

REPTILES

Fox snake	*Elaphe vulpina*
Snake	*See* Fox snake
Snapping turtle	*Chelydra serpentina*

FISH

Bass, Calico	*See* Crappie, Black; Crappie, White
Bass, Largemouth	*Micropterus salmoides*
Bass, Smallmouth	*Micropterus dolomieui*
Bluegill	*Lepomis macrochirus*
Bowfin	*Amia calva*
Carp	*Cyprinus carpio*
Carpsucker	*Carpiodes carpio*
	Carpiodes velifer
Catfish	Ictaluridae
Crappie, Black	*Pomoxis nigromaculatus*
Crappie, White	*Pomoxis annularis*
Dogfish	*See* Bowfin
Gar	*Lepisosteus platostomus*
	Lepisosteus osseus
Salmon	*Salmo* spp.
Sucker	Catastomidae
Sunfish	*Lepomis* spp.
Trout, Brook	*Salvelinus fontinalis*
Trout, Brown	*Salmo trutta*
Trout, Lake	*Salvelinus namaycush*
Trout, Rainbow	*Salmo gairdneri*
Whitefish	*Coregonus clupeaformis*

MAMMALS

Beaver	*Castor canadensis*
Cottontail	*Sylvilagus* spp.
Deer, White-tailed	*Odocoileus virginianus*
Hare, Snowshoe	*Lepus americanus*
Jackrabbit	*Lepus* spp.
Muskrat	*Ondatra zibethicus*
Opossum	*Didelphis virginiana*
Porcupine	*Erethizon dorsatum*
Raccoon	*Procyon lotor*
Rat	*See* Muskrat
Squirrel, Fox	*Sciurus niger*
Squirrel, Gray	*Sciurus carolinensis*
Squirrel, Ground	*Spermophilus* spp.
Squirrel, Red	*Sciurus hudsonicus*
Woodchuck	*Marmota* spp.

Baldpate	*See* Widgeon
Bittern	*Botaurus lentiginosus*
Bluebill	*See* Scaup, Greater; Scaup, Lesser
Bufflehead	*Bucephala albeola*
Canvasback	*Aythya valisneria*
Coot	*Fulica americana*
Crow	*Corvus brachyrhyncos*
Dove	*See* Mourning Dove
Dove, Rock	*Columba livia*
Duck, Black	*Anas rubipes*
Duck, Ring-necked	*Aythya collaris*
Duck, Wood	*Aix sponsa*
Gadwall	*Anas strepara*
Goldeneye	*Bucephala clangula*
	Bucephala islandica
Goose	Anserinae
Grouse, Ruffed	*Bonasa umbellus*
Grouse, Sharp-tailed	*Tympanuchus phasianellus*
Jacksnipe	*See* Snipe, Common
Mallard	*Anas platyrhynchos*
Merganser, Common	*Mergus merganser*
Merganser, Hooded	*Lophodytes cucullatus*
Mourning Dove	*Zenaidura macroura*
Oldsquaw	*Clangula hyemalis*
Partridge	*See* Grouse, Ruffed
Partridge, Gray	*Perdix perdix*
Partridge, Hungarian	*See* Partridge, Gray
Pheasant	*Phasianus colchicus*
Pigeon	*See* Dove, Rock
Pintail	*Anas acuta*
Rail	Rallinae
Redhead	*Aythya americana*
Scaup, Greater	*Aythya marila*
Scaup, Lesser	*Aythya affinis*
Scoter	*Melanitta* spp.
Sharptail	*See* Grouse, Sharp-tailed
Shoveller	*Anas clypeata*
Snipe, Common	*Capella gallinago*
Squab	*See* Dove, Rock
Starling	*Sturnus vulgaris*
Teal, Blue-winged	*Anas discors*
Teal, Green-winged	*Anas crecca*
Timberdoodle	*See* Woodcock
Widgeon	*Anas americana*
Woodcock	*Scolopax minor*

BIBLIOGRAPHY

American Ornithologists' Union. *Check-list of North American Birds,* 6th ed. Lawrence, Kansas: Amer. Ornithol. Union, 1983.

Becker, G. C. *Fishes of Wisconsin.* Madison: Univ. of Wisconsin Press, 1983.

Fernald, M. L. *Gray's Manual of Botany,* 8th ed. New York: American Book Co., 1950.

Gowanloch, J. N. *Fishes and Fishing in Louisiana.* Louisiana Dept. Cons. Bull. 23, 1933.

Gower, W. C. *The Use of the Bursa of Fabricius as an Indication of Age in Game Birds.* Trans. N. Amer. Wildl. Conf. 4:426–430, 1939.

Hobson, P. *Garden Way's Guide to Food Drying.* Charlotte, Vermont: Garden Way, 1980.

Hoffman, M. *Crockery Cookery.* New York: Bantam Books, 1975.

Jaycox, E. R. *Bee Keeping in Illinois.* Univ. of Illinois (Urbana/Champaign) College of Agriculture, U.S.D.A., and Univ. of Illinois Extension, 1969.

Kafka, B. *Microwave Gourmet.* New York: Morrow, 1987.

Kephart, H. *Camp Cookery.* New York: Macmillan, 1956.

Krieger, L. C. C. *The Mushroom Handbook.* New York: Dover Publications, 1967.

McKnight, K., and V. McKnight. *A Field Guide to Mushrooms.* Boston: Houghton Mifflin, 1987.

Nowak, R. M., and J. L. Paradiso. *Walker's Mammals of the World,* 4th ed. Baltimore: Johns Hopkins Univ. Press, 1983. 2 vols.

Peterson, L. *A Field Guide to Edible Wild Plants of Eastern and Central North America.* Boston: Houghton Mifflin, 1977.

Rhoades, R. *What Do You Mean— You Don't Like Turtle!* Ohio Cons. Bull. (Nov. 1950), 8–9, 29–30.

Smith, A. H. *Common Edible and Poisonous Mushrooms of Southeastern Michigan.* Cranbrook Inst. Sci. Bull. 14, 1938.

Smith, A. H. *The Mushroom Hunter's Field Guide.* Ann Arbor: Univ. of Michigan Press, 1971.

Smith, H. *The Master Book of Fish.* London: Spring Books, n.d.

Stevens, A. O. *Poisonous Plants and Plant Products.* North Dakota Agricultural College, Agric. Exper. Sta. Bull. 265, 1933.

Vogt, R. C. *Amphibians and Reptiles of Wisconsin.* Milwaukee: Milwaukee Public Museum, 1981.

Yanovsky, E. *Food Plants of the North American Indians.* U.S.D.A. Misc. Publ. 237, 1936.

INDEX

Boldface type indicates specific recipes or methods.